silver surfers'

COLOUR GUIDE TO travel & holidays

simon and susan veness

foulsham

LONDON • NEW YORK • TORONTO • SYDNEY

foulsham

The Publishing House, Bennetts Close, Cippenham,
Slough, Berkshire, SL1 5AP, England

Foulsham books can be found in all good bookshops and direct from
www.foulsham.com

ISBN: 978-0-572-03367-5

Cover photograph © Superstock

A CIP record for this book is available from the British Library

The moral rights of the authors have been asserted

While every effort has been made to ensure the
accuracy of all the information contained within this
book, neither the author nor the publisher can be liable
for any errors. In particular, since laws change from
time to time, it is vital that each individual checks
relevant legal details for themselves.

Printed in Dubai

Contents

Introduction

Get ready to travel the world – with the help of your computer! This book will tell you everything you need to know about getting to grips with travel online, via the world wide web and your PC.

In simple, easy-to-understand language and with all the confusing terminology explained, you can become your own online travel agent, researching everything you need to know about destinations, the best price (in total security), and where to stay when you are there.

The internet is the ideal way to arrange all your travel needs but it takes some getting used to and there are often 100 different ways to go about the same task. You can nearly always find what you are looking for, but sometimes it can take a while to track down if you don't start in the right place.

We have been working and researching online for the past ten years, so just relax and let us steer you through the fun – though potentially bewildering – world of internet travel.

What's in this book?

This is a step-by-step guide showing how to approach travel online, from your first ideas of where to go through the full booking process. It will make you confident in your choices, safe in your purchases and savvy in booking the holiday you want.

- Everything is set out in manageable sections, moving in a logical progression through the introductory steps, the research process, the booking process and other travel essentials.

- We don't assume any great familiarity with the internet in general and travel in particular.

- Key points will be repeated, so you don't need to memorise everything at once. Go at your own pace.

- We will provide plenty of practical, reassuring advice, as well as regular visual aids, examples, terminology and pertinent tips.

- Practice makes perfect! There will be plenty of opportunity to try out your new skills – and it's vital that you do.

How this book works

While you may be keen to get started straight away, you will need to read through the first three sections at least before you do, so don't get too ambitious too soon.

Pay special attention to the section on Price (in Chapter 6) and Buying Safely (Chapter 8), as these are essential to your peace of mind.

- The first three chapters are designed to give you all the basic internet skills you need to search confidently and quickly.

- Chapters 4–7 are designed to give you a full understanding of how online travel works, with all the key terminology, price points and specialist advice.

Surfing in the USA

Although this guide is designed primarily with the UK audience in mind, American readers can easily get the same benefits by using the US version of Google and Yahoo (**www. google.com** and **www.yahoo.com**), as well as looking for the US version of any websites earmarked specifically for the UK audience. Everyone, wherever they are, will find search results vary from those illustrated because websites are constantly changing, but the process of researching and booking remains the same.

- In chapters 8–12, we put all the lessons of the first seven chapters into practice and walk you through the exact 'How to do it' of finding the right holiday and booking it.

- Chapters 13–15 are geared purely around practical holiday advice, with all the necessary background to things like luggage, road maps and inoculations.

- Finally, we have a round-up chapter which provides an at-a-glance guide to all the key websites and reference tools.

Don't worry about all that information

There is a *massive* amount of information out there and it is easy to get sidetracked or baffled. Much of what you find will be advertising, which can generally be ignored.

Good words to know

Net, world wide web, or just the web: Terms for the vast database of knowledge and information sharing through millions of computers worldwide, linked together into a huge global network.

Online: Exploring the internet. Once you have an internet connection, you are 'online'.

What do you need to get started?

The first thing you need is a clear idea of what you are looking for. Have an outline plan of what you want from your destination, transportation and accommodation, then get a nice cup of tea, make yourself comfortable and begin searching.

If you are nervous about using the internet in the first place, Helen Brookes' masterful book, *Silver Surfers' Colour Guide to the Internet*, is a good resource to allay any initial fears.

Mastering the basics of internet use, like saving sites on your Favorites list and using the Back and Forward buttons to move between pages, are extremely helpful. We will give you a good grasp of the essentials without too much formal introduction.

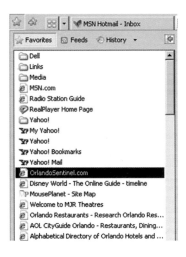

The bottom line is that it is increasingly important for people to be able to do their own holiday 'homework' as the traditional high street travel agent is likely to become a rare animal in the not too distant future.

Competition from online sources, low-cost airlines and other direct-sell tour operators have all combined to make the travel agent an endangered species, while you can usually save money by 'doing it yourself', as this obviously cuts out the middleman.

A recent report into internet usage forecast that 17 million people in Britain would book at least part of their main holiday online in 2007 and another 13 million would purchase part of a short break via the internet. More than 21 million are likely to seek information on their holiday choice from their computer, too.

Whichever way you slice it, that is a *lot* of people looking for a *lot* of information and spending a *lot* of money!

Don't worry **about different hotel chains**

As an example of travel confusion, negotiating your way through the vast maze of hotel chains is both time-consuming and unnecessary. Many are owned by the same overall company (Intercontinental Hotels Group, for example, own seven major brands including: Holiday Inn, Staybridge Suites and Crowne Plaza) so you can often save time by going to their main website and simply selecting your destination. Unless you have very strong feelings about sticking with one brand, you will usually get better value by shopping around.

However, don't go plunging head first into the wonderful world wide web without having an idea of that key ingredient, price. It is important to know the current market rate for anything before you commit your hard-earned cash to an online vendor, and that is especially true of travel.

Don't buy something simply because it promises you '50% off!' The starting price might have been artificially high, while a competitor might be offering 55%!

This is where the right search techniques and a little patience will pay off handsomely in the long term. Stick with us through the early chapters as we deal with the basics, then we will venture forth into the more complex and demanding world of online travel.

Right, are you sitting comfortably? Then we will begin ...

Chapter 1

Getting Started

Within the scope of this book, we assume you have a complete computer system, you know how to turn it on, how to establish an internet connection and how to use the keyboard, mouse and printer.

Terms you need to know before using the internet

Connections:

- **Dial-up connection:** A connection to the internet that runs through your phone line. A dial-up connection is like making a phone call. You cannot make or receive phone calls while connected to the internet via a dial-up connection. Transmission of data from the internet is slow.

- **DSL (Digital Subscriber Line):** A high-speed connection to the internet, that runs through your phone line. Unlike with a dial-up connection, you are still able to use your phone while connected to the internet.

- **Cable modem:** The box that connects your computer to the incoming internet connection supplied by your cable, satellite or TV company. Provides 'high-speed cable internet access'.

- **Broadband:** A general term for 'high-speed connection'.

Moving around:

- **Internet Explorer:** Microsoft's web browser that comes as a standard part of your Windows package.

- **Netscape:** An alternative web browser, similar to Internet Explorer, that comes with some Windows, Mac and UNIX packages.

Manipulating information:

- **Download:** The process of receiving or copying information from an online location to your computer, such as 'downloading' an upgrade for an existing program.

- **Upload:** The process of copying information from your computer on to the internet, such as 'uploading' pictures on to a picture storage website.

Don't worry about remembering everything

You do not have to memorise all the terms listed. Some of them are important (such as knowing what the Address bar is) but most of them will not affect your ability to use the internet. They are meant to be an overview of terms you will come across in the book, and are a quick reference if you need a reminder as you begin researching your holiday.

General terms:

- **Address bar:** The space, located at the upper left corner of your screen once you connect to the internet, in which you type a website address. Also known as the **Navigation bar** when using Netscape.

- **Surfing (or surfing the net):** Going from website to website on the internet.

Other good words to know

Browser: A computer program that fetches and displays internet web pages. To get on the net in the first place, you need to open your browser program (such as Internet Explorer).

Mac: Short for Macintosh computer.

Windows: The basic operating system on most PCs, such as Windows XP or Windows Vista.

- **Website:** A collection of documents or 'pages' available on the internet.

Before we start searching for that holiday of a lifetime, there are some basic precautions you must be aware of to navigate safely and with confidence.

Common-sense precautions

Just as you would use common sense while travelling to a foreign country, you must also be mindful of strangers and situations you might meet on the internet. Here are a few simple ways to stay safe during your internet travels.

- Never give out your passwords – never.

- Never give out personal information via e-mail, on an internet forum or on any unsecured site.

- Never open an e-mail, especially one with an attachment, if you do not know the sender. Delete it without opening.

- Never respond to e-mails asking for personal information.

- Keep your anti-virus, anti-spyware, firewall and spam programs running and updated.

- Disconnect from the internet or shut down your computer when not in use.

- Don't use the same password for every site you visit. Perhaps use one for forums, one for banking, one for purchases, etc.

- Don't believe everything you read on internet forums. Doing your own research is crucial.

Making online purchases presents its own set of safety issues. Again, it is easy to stay safe.

- Always check for the closed padlock icon at the bottom right side of your browser. A padlock icon on the website itself is meaningless. It must show up in your browser.

Good words to know

Anti-virus program: An essential program which scans and deletes any 'viruses' you may pick up from the internet or in e-mail.

Firewall: A security system that prevents unauthorised access to your PC from outside sources.

Spyware: Unwanted 'vandalism' from cyberspace; a good anti-spyware program will ensure hackers don't gain access to your computer info.

Use all three of the above together for maximum internet security.

Spam: The internet equivalent of junk mail – unsolicited e-mails.

• Look at the address in the Address bar. The 'http' at the beginning of the web address will automatically change to 'https', indicating the connection is now secure.

Choosing a secure password

Some passwords are more secure than others. How do you choose a safe one?

• Your password should not be something close friends or family members could guess. Your pet's name, your grandchild's name or your birth date are not secure passwords.

• Your password should not be something a hacker (internet hooligan) could quickly guess. Straightforward words or variations on words ('password' or 'p@ssw0rd') are easy to guess.

- Secure passwords are composed of eight or more characters, include random numbers, symbols and both upper and lower case letters.

But it's hard to remember random combinations. How do you make it secure and memorable?

- Think of a phrase that has meaning for you: 'I love to travel with my cat'.

- Shorten it into letters, numbers and symbols: Ilv2TwmC@.

- If that seems too daunting, choose a nonsense string of words and symbols (snoot54&tinker2). This is less memorable, but more secure than choosing something obvious like 'Betty123'.

Don't worry about writing it down

In a perfect world, you should not write your passwords down. However, memory isn't always perfect and it's better to keep your passwords in a safe place than to forget them and not be able to access your accounts. If possible, just write down the first few characters or a clue as a 'hint' to yourself. If necessary, write them down in full and hide them well.

For more on safe surfing visit: **www.getsafeonline.org.uk**.

Your reminder box

- Become familiar with some basic computer and internet terms, but don't feel you must memorise them.

- A closed padlock and the designation 'https' indicate the website has become secure and will encrypt your personal information.

- Create a safe password, making sure you can remember what it is.

- Never give anyone your password. This cannot be stressed enough.

Chapter 2

Finding Things Out

Having access to the internet is like being given a library card for the biggest library in the universe, only to discover all the books have been placed randomly on the shelves, you can't find the card catalogue and the librarian seems to have gone home for the day!

Using the internet as an information resource

Rest assured, there *is* a librarian on duty 24 hours a day – several of them, in fact. They are known as search engines and directories.

Good words to know

Search directory: A tool, similar to a search engine, which utilises real people to assign the priority of the web pages corresponding to your search terms rather than assigning priority based on keywords. This process is less accurate than a search engine as new sites are often not added to the directory for some time. Directories also use categories to assist you in searching. Yahoo directory is an example of a directory. A book's table of contents is similar to a directory's list.

Search engine: A tool that allows you to enter words or terms ('keywords') into the Search box, searches for web pages that are most relevant to the keyword or terms you entered into the box, then provides a comprehensive list of suitable web addresses. Google is an example of a search engine. A book's index is similar to a search engine's list.

The difference between search engines and directories

The difference is obvious when you compare Google and Yahoo directories. First let's look at Google.

- Open a browser window by double clicking on the **Internet Explorer** (or **Netscape Navigator**) icon on your desktop.

- Highlight the current address in your Address bar by clicking on it.

- Type www.google.co.uk into the Address bar.

- Click the **Go** button or press the **Enter** key on your keyboard.

Google's main page appears, with an empty box in the middle of the page. This box is where you will type your search terms.

Don't worry **about clicking Go**

Pressing the **Enter** key on your keyboard is quicker and easier and serves the same purpose as clicking **Search** or **Go** when you enter a new address into your Address bar.

Now let's look at the Yahoo Directory.

- Highlight **www.google.com** in your Address bar by clicking on it.

- Type in dir.yahoo.com (do not type www. first).

- Press **Enter** on your keyboard.

- The list showing on the left-hand side of the screen is the Yahoo Directory.

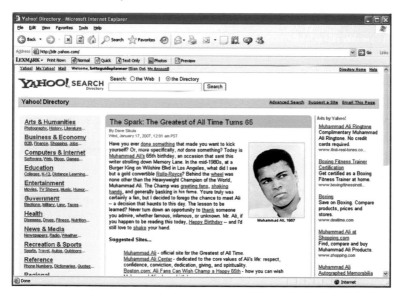

- By clicking on a category (Recreation & Sports) or subcategory (Travel) you are taken to a new list specific to that topic.

Entertainment
Movies, TV Shows, Music, Humor...

Government
Elections, Military, Law, Taxes...

Health
Diseases, Drugs, Fitness, Nutrition...

News & Media
Newspapers, Radio, Weather...

Recreation & Sports
Sports, Travel, Autos, Outdoors...

- Clicking on a new category within the new list narrows your search to a number of relevant websites.

Additional Categories

- **Air Travel** (71)
- **Automotive** (248)
- **Backpacking** (26)
- **Boating@**
- **Booksellers@**
- **Budget Travel** (18)
- **Business Travel** (7)
- **Chats and Forums** (19)
- **Civilian Space Travel@**
- **Companion Services** (5)
- **Cruises** (58)
- **Currency Exchange Rates@**
- **Destination Guides** (32539) NEW!
- **Directories@**
- **Disabilities@**
- **Ecotourism** (19)
- **Family Travel** (24)
- **Health and Medicine@**
- **Hitchhiking** (8)

- **Maps@**
- **News and Media** (155)
- **Ongoing Travelogues@**
- **Organizations** (11)
- **Photos** (1310)
- **Publishers@**
- **Resorts@**
- **Seniors** (11)
- **Software@**
- **Tour Operators@**
- **Tourism Research@**
- **Train Travel** (20)
- **Transportation** (2667)
- **Travel Agents@**
- **Travel Tips and Tools** (82)
- **Travel Writing@**
- **Traveling Alone** (12)
- **Traveling With Pets@**
- **Travelogues** (1564) NEW!

- Click on a link that suits your needs and you will be taken to that website.

Another directory you may wish to try can be found at **www.directory.co.uk**. Browse topics on the main page or enter search terms into the box at the top.

Yahoo also functions as a search engine

- Highlight the current address in the Address bar by clicking on it.

- Type www.yahoo.com into the Address bar.

- Press the **Enter** key.

- Yahoo's main page comes up, with a Search box at the top and an index along the left-hand side.

We will use search engines and directories again in the next chapter, but there are other valuable online tools to help you research your travel needs.

Other useful research tools

Straightforward search tools are invaluable, but they are more about function than fun. Several online research tools are also entertaining and can be fairly addictive. Because they tend to have their own unique 'flavour', it is worth searching for sites that match your personality and sense of adventure.

You will learn the specifics of using each of these resources in Chapter 9. For now, let's have a brief overview.

Tourist offices

Tourism offices include government tourism offices, ministries of tourism, chambers of commerce and visitor and convention bureaux, and are often a great starting point when researching your holiday destination. Official tourism offices provide free, unbiased travel information for their particular destination, including attractions, shopping, dining, recreation and more.

Travel forums

Travel forums (discussion boards) are an excellent resource for researching specifics about your travel destination. Forums allow you to ask questions and receive answers from real travellers with real experience. Bear in mind though that opinions vary and, because anyone can post their thoughts, not all the information on an internet forum will be correct.

Don't worry **about membership**

You do not have to register as a member to view messages on an internet forum. However, if you want to post a question you must register first (see pages 141–2). Always read the forum's Guidelines For Posting page or Forum Rules before posting.

Blogs

The word Blog is a shortened version of Web Log and refers to personal online diaries or journals maintained by an individual or group. Travel blogs give readers a glimpse into the author's travel experiences, both good and bad. They often include pictures and links to other relevant web pages.

Don't worry **about plug-ins**

You may be required to download programs such as Musicmatch Jukebox or RealPlayer to hear podcasts, or Shockwave Flash to see videos or view webcams. These programs, called plug-ins, are safe and free. If you need the program, a pop-up box will prompt you to download it.

Podcasts

Podcast is a blending of 'iPod' and 'broadcast', and refers to a digital recording of an audio broadcast which can be downloaded (free) to a personal audio player such as an iPod, or through your computer via the internet. Think of it as a mini audio documentary or an audio version of The Travel Channel.

Your reminder box

- Search engines are a quick way of finding what you want on the web, using keywords to narrow your options.

- Directories help narrow your focus, using lists sorted into specific categories.

- Pressing the **Enter** key on your keyboard performs the same action as clicking **Search** or **Go** using your mouse.

- Don't forget to use 'fun' research tools, such as blogs.

Chapter 3

Search Skills

Before you can utilise the online tools available for researching your travel needs, you must know what your travel needs are. Depending on the sort of holiday you are looking for, you are likely to need the basics: accommodation, transportation to and from your destination, and possibly car hire.

In addition, you may want attraction tickets, dining reservations, shopping information and general travel advice relevant to your destination. They can all be found online, once you know how to track them down.

Using search engines

You are finally ready to begin researching your holiday. Now, how do you find what you're looking for in seemingly endless cyberspace? This is where search engines and directories come in.

The two biggest search engines are Google (**www.google.com** or **www.google.co.uk** for UK-specific options) and Yahoo (**www.yahoo.com** or **www.yahoo.co.uk**). If you are using a Microsoft product (Windows), **MSN.co.uk** will be your default search engine, but you can add Google or Yahoo to your Favorites list (see pages 35–39 for step-by-step instructions) and link to your preferred search engine that way.

Don't worry about sponsored links

Whenever you do a Google search, you may find the first few responses appear in a blue-tinted panel and are not necessarily representative of your search. These are sponsored links and are of varying value. For the top genuine search choice, you may need to go down two or three results (see the Cirque du Soleil example on the following page).

Let's search Google for tickets to Cirque du Soleil.

* Open a new browser window (by double clicking on the **Internet Explorer/Netscape Navigator** icon on your desktop).

* Type www.google.co.uk into your browser window and press **Enter**. This is the page you will see:

* Type "Cirque du Soleil" (the use of quotation marks is important – see the section on Refining your search terms, below) into the empty Search box.

* Press **Enter**.

* Notice the first two sites are ticket brokers not affiliated with Cirque du Soleil and the third site is in French.

* Scan the list until you see Cirque du Soleil's website address at the bottom of the description.

* Click on the **Cirque du Soleil official website** link.

* The ticket drop-down menu appears on the left-hand side of Cirque's main page.

Don't worry **about getting different results**

When you try this exercise for yourself you are very likely to get different results to those shown in the illustrations. This is true for all the exercises and illustrations in this book, which show a 'snapshot' of the information on the internet at a specific point in time. Because the internet is constantly changing – new sites are always being added and information is being updated – your results may well be different, but the same principles will apply.

If you see several websites you think are worth exploring, you can keep the search results window open while you visit a selected link by doing the following:

- Follow the previous instructions until you reach the results page.

- Place your curser over the link to **Cirque du Soleil official website**.

- Instead of left-clicking, click the button on the right side of your mouse (right click).

- A pop-up box will appear.

- Left click on **Open in New Window**.

- A new browser window will open automatically, showing Cirque du Soleil's website.

We will remind you of both options at various points throughout the book. Feel free to decide which method you prefer.

There's more!

Google's search engine also does calculations and conversions quickly and easily – for example, currency conversions and Fahrenheit/Celsius conversions. Type 2 miles into a Google Search box and it returns the calculation 3.218688 kilometres. Type in quarter cup in tablespoons and it returns the conversion 4 US tablespoons.

More search engines:

- **www.uk.ask.com** or **www.ask.com** Search engine and directory that deals especially well with phrases as search terms.

- **www.ixquick.com** Uses several other search engines to prioritise results.

- **www.msn.co.uk** or **www.msn.com** Window's default search engine.

- **www.net.gurus.com/search** Provides links to other search engines.

- **www.search-engines-megalist.com** Every search engine known to humankind, but with a tedious list to wade through.

- **www.toorista.com/en** Travel-specific search engine and directory.

There are hundreds of search engines available, some travel-specific (such as **aardvarktravel.net** and **travoogle.com**), but we find most of them are cumbersome to use and inaccurate in their results. Don't be afraid to try different engines, though. The worst that can happen is a wasted minute or two.

Using directories

Using Yahoo Directory, let's search for a canal boat cruise.

- Open a new browser window.

- Type dir.yahoo.com (do not type www. first) in the Address bar.

- Press **Enter**.

- Scan the list that appears down the left side of the browser window until you see the main heading, Recreation & Sports. Underneath the main heading, find the subheading Travel.

Yahoo! Directory

Arts & Humanities
Photography, History, Literature...

Business & Economy
B2B, Finance, Shopping, Jobs...

Computers & Internet
Software, Web, Blogs, Games...

Education
Colleges, K-12, Distance Learning...

Entertainment
Movies, TV Shows, Music, Humor...

Government
Elections, Military, Law, Taxes...

Health
Diseases, Drugs, Fitness, Nutrition...

News & Media
Newspapers, Radio, Weather...

Recreation & Sports
Sports, Travel, Autos, Outdoors...

- Click on the **Travel** link.

- Scan the list until you see Cruises.

  - **Civilian Space Travel@**
  - **Companion Services** (5)
  - **Cruises** (58)
  - **Currency Exchange Rates@**
  - **Destination Guides** (32539) **NEW!**

- Click on the **Cruises** link.

- Under Consumer Categories, click on the **Shopping and Services@** link.

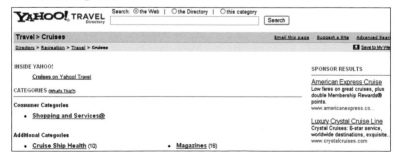

28

- Several more categories will appear. Click on **Barge Cruises**.

- The list generated provides links to specific websites dealing with barge cruises. Reading the descriptions below each link will give you an idea of what area the website covers and what sort of cruises they offer.

- Click on the **Go Barging** link under Site Listings.

- The GoBarging website appears.

Directories involve a lot of work for the same result you would get using a search engine. However, if you aren't sure what to look for or if your search terms are not yielding good results, then a directory can help narrow your focus.

Don't worry about an inactive back button

You may click on a link that takes you to a new web page, but when you want to return to the page you were previously viewing the **Back** button doesn't work. The website you are currently viewing popped up in a new browser window. Click on the red X in the upper right-hand corner. The original website is 'hiding' behind the new window.

More directories:

- **www.dmoz.org** Open Directory project.
- **www.google.com/dirhp** Google's directory.
- **www.toorista.com/en** Travel-specific directory.

Refining your search terms

Enter the keyword travel into a Google Search box and it will retrieve 773,000,000 relevant links. Obviously, refining the search is necessary or you will still be wading through websites long after your holiday dates have come and gone. Enter travel United States and you're down to 194,000,000 links. Narrow your search further by typing travel United States Florida and only 13,600,000 pages match those terms. The search terms are still too broad to be of any real use. There are better ways to refine, quickly and easily.

Enclosing your terms in quotation marks

Let's say you want to visit Clearwater, Florida for a dolphin sighting cruise.

- Type in Clearwater Florida dolphin cruises and you get 172,000 pages, with the first results being about resorts in Clearwater Florida.

- By adding quotation marks around the specific thing you are looking for, with the location outside quotes "dolphin cruises" Clearwater Florida you get 334 pages, the first three being specific dolphin cruise companies.

- Type in a specific dolphin cruise company "Dolphin Landings" Clearwater Florida and you get 157 links.

Don't worry about connectors and punctuation

Search engines assume punctuation and connecting words ('and', 'the', 'as', 'or'). You do not have to type them as part of your search terms.

But, just to make it more complicated, in this case Dolphin Landings' actual website link doesn't show up on the first page. There are 16 websites listed before Dolphin Landings' own site. There must be a better way. And there is.

- Type in the name "Dolphin Landings" in quotation marks, and there they are, right at the top of the list. Why? The extra qualifiers (Clearwater Florida) are sometimes too broad. Then again, sometimes they aren't.

- Try the same approaches with "Boggy Creek Airboats" Kissimmee Florida and they're right at the top of the list every time, with or without quotations. Sometimes you just have to experiment.

Don't worry **about quotation marks**

An ineffective placement of quotation marks will be immediately obvious. Your search will return results that don't meet your needs, or you will get an error page. But don't worry! It happens to the most seasoned of search pros – often – and is simply a matter of trying different combinations until you get a satisfactory result.

What if you get results unrelated to your topic? Check your spelling. If you entered Nassah as your search term, you may be confused when a family-owned electrical business tops the results list. Fortunately, Google and Yahoo offer the gentle query 'Did you mean: Nassau?' at the top of the list, providing a new search under the correct spelling just by clicking on the word **Nassau**.

Did you mean: *nassau*

NASSAH Services Ltd.
Nassah Services Ltd. is a family business that has been active in the electrical contracting industry for over 25 years, we are also active in the Audio ...
www.nassahservices.co.uk/ - 7k - Cached - Similar pages

Using search engines can be a bit of an art form. Your search terms will become more precise (and more creative) the more you use search engines.

Specific language searches

Let's say Musée d'Orsay is on your list of attractions to visit in Paris, France. Typing the term Musee d'Orsay results in several links, all of which are in French. Short of learning French quickly, what can you do?

- You may be offered the option: [**Translate this page**]. Some websites have versions in several languages and you may be taken to your default language within the website (your computer 'knows' if you are using English, French, German, etc.).

- The page may route through an actual translator program, with varying (and sometimes hilarious) degrees of success.

<u>musée d'orsay</u>- [<u>Translate this page</u>]
Présentation du musée et des collections (1848-1914). Programme des expositions temporaires et des événements culturels associés. Animations pédagogiques ...
www.musee-orsay.fr/ - 8k - <u>Cached</u> - <u>Similar pages</u>
    <u>Bienvenue sur le site du</u> - www.musee-orsay.fr/ORSAY/orsayNews/HTML.NSF/By...
    <u>welcome to Musée d'Orsay (...</u> - www.musee-orsay.fr/ORSAY/orsaygb/HTML.NSF...
    <u>Editorial</u> - www.musee-orsay.fr/.../HTML.NSF/VLien/Evenement?openDocument
    <u>More results from www.musee-orsay.fr »</u>

- When using Google, look for the link at the bottom right-hand side of the Search box, labelled **Language Tools**.

- Click on the link and you will have the option to search only for pages in the language of your choice, as well as tools to translate specific text or entire web pages.

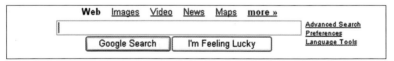

Picture and image searches

Yahoo and Google give you the option to search for images simply by clicking on the Images link above the Search box.

- Type in your search term. Instead of a links list your search returns the images requested.

- Click on the picture of your choice and it takes you directly to the website that photo is posted on.

Want to see pictures of Tower Bridge?

- Click **Images** above the Google Search box.

- Type "Tower Bridge" in the Search box.

- Press **Enter**.

- Google returns more than 100,000 images.

- Type in "Tower Bridge at night" and Google returns nearly 3,500 night-time shots.

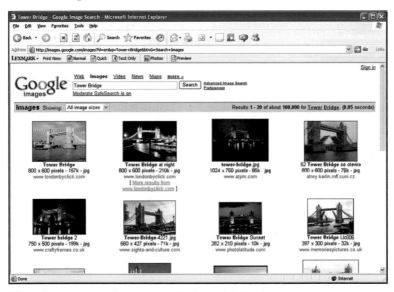

This feature can be particularly useful when you want to see what a resort hotel room looks like but the resort website does not include pictures.

- Click **Images** above the Google Search box.

- Type "Hotel Splendido Portofino" in the Search box.

- Press **Enter**.

- Google returns five images, two of which are pictures of suites.

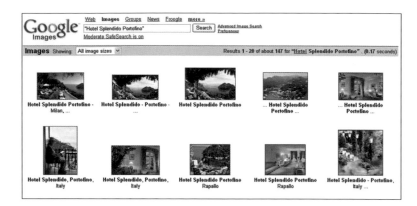

• A Yahoo search returns four results. Try both search engines, as their images are different.

Don't worry about extra links

You may notice a column along the right-hand side of the search results page with titles like 'Buy Nile Cruises' and 'Everything You Want To Know About Nile Cruises'. This right-hand column is a list of advertisements, shown in order of how much money the company was willing to pay to have their advert at the top of the list. Sometimes they are useful, but be aware that they are sales tools and will not necessarily have information about your topic.

Search errors

When you click on a link in your search results you will occasionally get an error message e.g. **404 Error: File Not Found**, or **Page Cannot Be Displayed**. This happens when the link to the page has been broken in some way. Often, the website has shut down, the particular page has moved or no longer exists, or the website is doing maintenance. Try again right away, as it sometimes occurs due to a transmission error. If you get the error message again, try at a later date.

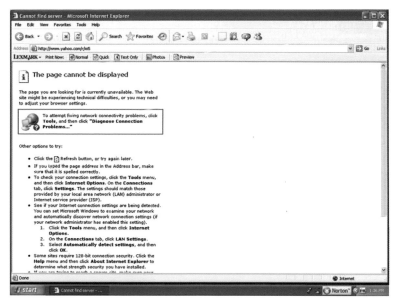

You will also get the Page Cannot Be Displayed message when you have lost your connection to the internet. Try visiting another site to see if your connection is still working. If another website comes up, your connection is active and it is likely the website that generated the error message has moved or is currently unavailable.

Managing your searches

The more you search, the more fascinating websites you'll find and the more information you'll want to store for later reference or repeated use. Web addresses can be easily 'bookmarked' by adding them to Favorites.

Storing favourite addresses using Internet Explorer

In this example we will store **Expedia.co.uk** in your Favorites list.

• Open a browser window using Internet Explorer.

• Type www.expedia.co.uk in the Address bar.

Good words to know

Favorites (note American spelling) or **Bookmarks:** Your personal list of 'saved' internet sites, the ones you like to visit on a regular basis.

Menu bar: The bar at the top of your screen displaying various tasks such as File, Edit and View.

Pop-ups: Small windows that 'pop up' unsolicited on some web pages, usually advertisements or sales offers.

Standard Buttons bar: The row of icons below the Menu bar, which allow you to perform various functions with one click (Back, Search, Home, Favorites). Also called the Toolbar.

• Press **Enter**.

• Once Expedia.co.uk's website appears in your browser window, look for the Favorites tab in the Standard Buttons bar at the top of your screen.

• Click once on **Favorites** or the star-plus symbol with Internet Explorer 7.

• A drop-down menu will appear along the left side of your screen.

• Click the **Add** button or the **Add to favorites** tab (with Internet Explorer 7).

• A pop-up will appear with Expedia.co.uk's description in the Name box.

- Click **OK** or **Add** to add the link to your Favorites.

When you want to access that link again, simply click on the Favorites tab in your Standard Buttons bar and the list of links you have saved will appear down the left-hand side of your screen.

Bookmarking favourite links using Netscape Navigator

- Open a browser window and type www.expedia.co.uk into your Address bar.

- Press **Enter**.

- Click once on **Bookmarks**. A menu will appear.

- Click once on **Bookmark This Page** to add the link to your list.

- To access the link again later, click once on **Bookmarks** and your saved website list will appear.

Managing your Favorites list

It is likely that your Favorites list will quickly become unwieldy and need to be organised. By creating folders within your Favorites list, you can group similar websites together under one heading, making it easier to find exactly what you're looking for.

When comparison shopping for flights, accommodation and car hire, having several links to online travel agents (such as Expedia) will be essential. With that in mind, let's create a folder called Travel Agents.

- Open a browser window using Internet Explorer.

- Click on **Favorites** in your Standard Buttons bar.

- Click on **Organize** (again, American spelling), next to the Add button on the Favorites drop-down menu.

- A pop-up box will appear. Look for the Create Folder button on the left side.

- Click on the **Create Folder** button.

- A box with a yellow folder will appear at the bottom of your existing favorites links (the window on the right side of the Organize Favorites box), entitled New Folder. There will be a flashing cursor inside the box.

- Type Travel Agents in the New Folder box.

- Click the **Close** button.

Moving existing links into folders

The technique used to move a link into a folder is called 'drag and drop'. This is how it works:

- Open a browser window and click on the **Favorites** button.

- Place your cursor over the link you want to move into a folder.

- The link will change colour and become underlined, indicating it is now active.

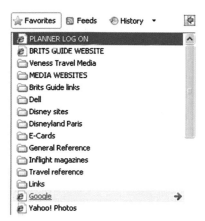

- Press the left button on your mouse, holding it down rather than clicking it quickly.

- While still holding the left button down, move your cursor to the folder you wish to place the link in.

- When the link is directly over the folder, let go of the left button.

- This will insert the link inside the folder.

When you have your links filed in their proper folders, click on the folder once to open it and access the links.

Don't worry about dropping the link

If you drop the link as you are moving it towards the folder you wish to place it in, simply follow the steps again. It may either have dropped where you let go of the left button or have returned to its original location. If you don't see it right away, look further down your list.

Dealing with pop-ups

Your internet program should have a Pop-Up Blocker which you can switch on to stop most of these annoying advertisements.

- Click on **Tools** on the Menu bar.

- Click on **Pop-up Blocker** in the drop-down menu.

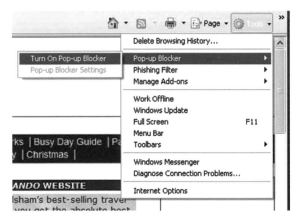

- Click on **Turn On Pop-up Blocker**.

You may want to allow pop-ups in some cases. When a web page you want to view is blocked as a pop-up, you will be prompted to temporarily allow pop-ups. Go ahead and click **Allow**.

Knowing when you've finished

With so much information available it can be difficult knowing when to stop searching. If the search is half the fun for you, keep going until you are satisfied you have seen enough. As a general rule, the following steps will give you a fairly representative sampling of what is available:

- Gather information and travel advice from at least one online tourist office for the area you will be visiting.

- Comparison shop between three or four booking sites (e.g. Expedia, Kayak, ebookers).
- Check prices on specific airline, hotel, car hire or tour operator websites.

Your reminder box

- Directories help you find what you want using a series of categories.
- Search engines help you find what you want using keywords.
- Enclose your search terms in quotation marks.
- Right click over a link to open it in a new browser window.
- Use specific search terms whenever possible.
- Click on the **Language Tool** to view only the pages available in a specific language.
- Find images quickly by using the Image link above the Google or Yahoo Search box.
- If the address you are using results in an Error message, check your internet connection.
- To save a website link, open your Favorites list and click the **Add** button.
- To save web links when using Netscape Navigator, open Bookmarks and click on **Bookmark This Page**.
- Use the 'drag and drop' technique to move links into folders.

Chapter 4

The Importance of Planning

Having ensured you have a good understanding of your computer and internet basics before heading out on the information superhighway, it is just as important to have a clear understanding of your travel requirements.

What am I looking for?

As you decide what to search for in the planning phase, be precise in your requirements. This will help to define what you are looking for and avoid unnecessary searches and frustration. While the internet is a terrific source of information, it can overwhelm you with choice and distractions, so stay focused on what you are looking for and avoid the temptation to click on the many associated sites that usually come up in conjunction with your search results.

It is also easy to be carried away by the enticing deals and packages that adorn virtually every travel website, plus the inevitable e-mail offers that arrive in your Inbox as soon as you register on some sites (see below for Should I register ...?).

• Start by setting out a rough budget for your travel needs. If your total budget for a long weekend for two in Prague is £500, and you are booking all the elements separately (flights, accommodation, transport/transfers) you can immediately rule out flights that will blow your budget from the outset. Review your budget after getting several online quotes.

• You also need to have a clear idea of the duration of your trip.

• Select your preferred mode of travel and note any requirements you might have, such as direct, non-stop flights rather than those involving at least one change en route.

- Check if your package includes transfers to and from the destination airport or if you will need a taxi or car hire – sometimes car hire can be the cheaper option.

- Will you rely on public transport and local excursions to get around, or will you need taxis if you don't hire a car? Try to check a few prices in advance so you don't get caught out by additional transport costs.

The essential message is to be prepared. Take your time and do your homework on the destinations that interest you *before* you book anything. The internet is the ideal tool for gathering

---

Should I register for information on various travel websites?

We tend to steer clear of websites that require us to register before we can access their information, or which offer special deals if you provide your e-mail address. All that tends to happen is your Inbox fills up with rubbish, much of which has nothing directly to do with your interest in flights, cruises, etc. This is because many sites sell their databases of e-mail addresses to other companies who then use them for indiscriminate e-mail shots – the internet equivalent of junk mail. However, if you don't mind sorting the wheat from the chaff, there are instances where you get genuinely useful information and offers. Many low-cost airlines are good at providing advance sale notices if you subscribe, while Expedia and Travelocity also have worthwhile subscriber-based e-mail lists. Here, you just enter your e-mail address in the box provided and click the **Subscribe** button.

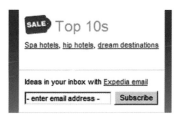

SALE Top 10s

Spa hotels, hip hotels, dream destinations

Ideas in your inbox with Expedia email

| - enter email address - | Subscribe |

information and you can find everything you need to make an informed decision.

Pay special attention

Three's company when it comes to getting estimates for things like flights, car hire and hotels. Usually you need at least three sample prices to be able to gauge what is – and isn't – a good deal.

Establishing a sequence for finding information

There are a number of ways to ensure you cover all your bases when searching for online travel. However, over the years we have put together a system which should work for just about everyone and is relatively simple to follow. The basic sequence is this:

Destination

The *where* of your holiday/travel choice is the most important and requires the most research. You need to ascertain exactly what your chosen destination has on offer. For this, you usually need three principal sources of information (as discussed in Chapters 2 and 3):

• The main tourist board for the area you are interested in.

• A good independent website covering that destination e.g. Columbus City Guides at **www.worldtravelguide.net**.

• A discussion forum offering up-to-the-minute advice.

Transport

The *how to get there* will require some of the more tedious price searching to work out the best deals and ensure you find the best way. For this you will need to look up at least some of the following:

• Flights.

• Airport.

- Rail travel.

- Road routes.

- Cruise/ferry lines.

- Bus/coach companies.

Accommodation

The *where to stay* element of your trip requires another few checks to be sure of what you are getting before you buy:

- The hotel's own website.

- An independent website like TripAdviser.com for real visitor reviews.

- A discussion forum for up-to-the-minute advice.

Car hire/public transport

You must ensure you can get around easily once you are there, so you need to consider whether you want to hire a car or use public transport/taxis. So you should check:

- Car hire prices.

- Public transport options (from the tourist board website).

- A rough idea of taxi prices.

Transfers

If you are not hiring a car and are not on a package holiday which arranges transportation, you will need to make arrangements for getting to and from the airport when you arrive in your destination. Therefore you should also check:

- The airport website for your options.

- Taxi prices.

- Any shuttle services that operate specifically from the airport to local hotels.

- Bus/coach options.

How does a package or DIY affect my choices?

To a large extent, the type of holiday or travel you are trying to find will influence the way you look for information, so there are generally two further ways to go about establishing a logical and user-friendly way of finding what you are after.

Good words to know

Package holiday: It may seem obvious, but a holiday 'package' is anything that combines the various transport and accommodation elements. Typically, a package holiday to, for example, the Costa del Sol will include your flights, hotel and transfers from the destination airport to and from your hotel. Some operators charge extra for transfers.

DIY holiday: This is our term for doing it yourself online. This way, you find and book your own flights or other transport, accommodation, car hire and any transfers separately, hence a DIY approach.

Package holidays

Just as your local High Street travel agent would be your first stop in the hunt for a typical package in the past, so there are a number of online travel agents offering the same kind of service. All the established travel agents now have an online 'shop', while new agents – like LastMinute, Expedia, ebookers and TravelSupermarket – have sprung up as an internet-only presence.

At the same time, the tour operators themselves (Virgin Holidays, Airtours, Thomson, Leger, etc) also now aim to sell direct to the consumer, hence both sources will offer a range of package holidays. That means your travel agent choice is wider than ever.

Don't worry **about all the names**

There's no need to try to work out who all these companies are or how they fit into the overall travel scene. Our final chapter on Useful Sites provides a comprehensive list of all the sites you *really* need to know about. As long as you have the web addresses, you are ready to travel!

Your regular sequence for finding a package deal will obviously be simpler (and rather less time consuming) than the DIY method, so the basic steps will be as follows:

- Establish your holiday requirements (when you want to go, what resort or destination you are looking for, how long you want to stay and how much you want to do in terms of sightseeing).

- Do your research (remember, the internet is now your travel agent).

- Make sure your travel insurance is up to date and you are covered for any unusual activities you might want to try, like horse riding, sailing, etc.

Let's consider the pros and cons of opting for a package arrangement.

Advantages: Most of the work is done for you and you should be fully covered if the operator fails for any reason.

Pay special attention

In most online packages (and even on flight-only bookings) you need to keep an eye out for sneaky 'extras' added on to the cost, like travel insurance. Very often you need to click **No** on a box or un-tick a 'Yes' box to avoid these unnecessary add-ons. We strongly advise you to take out a proper travel insurance policy that covers you for all the main eventualities (see Chapter 14).

Good words to know

The various online travel companies tend to use the same terminology when it comes to searching and buying their products. Some are obvious, others not so obvious. Some to watch out for include:

Cancellation fee: If you change or cancel a secured booking, there is usually an administrative fee.

e-brochures: The online version of traditional holiday brochures.

Minimum stay: The minimum number of nights you must book to get a reservation. Some flights and/or accommodation require a stay of a certain number of nights during busier times and may also specify that this must include a Friday or Saturday night.

Secured booking: A confirmed booking that you have made online, indicating you have paid at least a deposit.

Supplements: Additional costs for things like fuel charges, single occupancy of a double room, local taxes and surcharges or travelling at a peak time. For flights, some supplements can also include meals, checked luggage and pre-booked seats.

Tour operator: The actual provider of your holiday or travel, for example British Airways Holidays.

Travel agent: The 'shop' where you buy your travel requirements, either in the high street or online, for example, First Choice.

Unsecured or tentative booking: No pre-payment arranged. You are not committed to paying for the room/flight/car hire and there is no cancellation fee, but the room/flight/car hire can also be re-sold and the price changed.

Disadvantages: It may be cheaper to book all the elements yourself and packages have less flexibility with dates, resorts, etc. You often have only one flight choice (with a charter rather than a scheduled airline) and a limited range of accommodation. Most packages are also geared for one, two or sometimes three weeks. If you want to go for 6, 10 or 17 days, you will often be out of luck.

Do-it-yourself travel

This is where the internet really comes into its own. With patience, a little time and the right searching expertise, you really can put together your own package – often at a cheaper price than you would have got from a high street travel agent.

Many companies now offer a discount if you book online, which obviously produces an immediate saving and, while it is a more time-consuming process, you will also find more background information along the way.

You must go through a more involved sequence for DIY holidays and each one will depend on what kind of travel you are looking for.

- Once again, establish your holiday requirements first.

- Do your holiday research.

- If you are booking transport-only (flights, coach or rail travel), this is easiest to deal with by using your preferred search engine. Just search, ascertain the best price and book.

- When you are booking transport and accommodation, make sure the accommodation is available for your required dates before booking the transport.

- Once you have transport and accommodation booked, you should book any other travel incidentals that go with them (airport transfers or car hire).

- Use tourist board websites to ascertain what activities, events, shows and attractions are of interest to you and be ahead of the crowds by booking them in advance online.

- If you are feeling confident with your new-found search abilities, you can even make bookings for some restaurants online, too.

• Make sure your travel insurance is up to date and you are covered for any unusual activities you might want to try.

Pay special attention

In both package and DIY instances, it is vital you review everything you have ordered *before* you click **Confirm Booking** or **Buy Now**. In particular, check names are spelled correctly (and they *exactly* match your passports) and the dates are right (some American sites put the month before the date, for example, so that a date of 6 July 2007 which would be displayed in Europe as 06/07/07 would be 07/06/07 on an American calendar). In most cases, travel companies will not refund an erroneous booking without some kind of cancellation or administrative fee, so it's important to be sure of your order before you commit to paying.

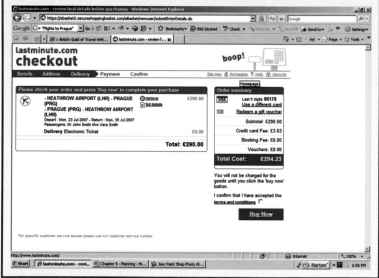

Advantages: With the DIY approach, you will have greater flexibility and control of your holiday and you can often save money, especially to non-resort destinations. Great for short breaks in particular. You can book any length of stay you want – you are not limited to the usual one or two-week tour operator choice.

Disadvantages: There are more elements of your holiday to co-ordinate and you need to make sure all are available for the dates you want before you book. If one element fails, you may not be covered to recover your costs for the others (if you lose your flight at the last minute, you may still have to pay for the other pre-booked elements like accommodation).

Tickets and attractions

In most instances, people arrive fairly unprepared for their holiday in their chosen destination. However, with the aid of the internet, you can be several steps ahead of the majority by taking some time to see what's available.

When it comes to DIY, you really can plan and book things almost to the *nth* degree by looking up all the activities and attractions in advance.

There are well-established ticket brokers you can visit to book shows, museums, sporting events and other attractions, while the tourist boards for cities, states and countries will provide fairly comprehensive lists of what is available.

UK ticket brokers

Airport Parking and Hotels: (**www.aph.com/information/attraction_tickets.htm**) Offers ticket services to worldwide destinations like Orlando, New York, Las Vegas, Barcelona, Paris and London.

Attraction Tickets Direct: (**www.attraction-tickets-direct.co.uk**) Another wide variety of ticket and sightseeing choices, specialising in Orlando and Florida but also including California, New York, Las Vegas, Hawaii, Toronto, Canada, parts of Europe, Dubai, South Africa, Hong Kong and Australia. They also feature useful information and discussion forums.

Attraction World: (**www.attractionworld.com**) Handles tickets for Florida, New York, West Coast USA, Europe and Britain.

Keith Prowse Attraction Tickets: (www.keithprowsetickets. com) A terrific variety of attraction tickets, shows and sightseeing for Britain (especially London), USA (especially Florida and California), France (especially Paris), Spain, Austria, the Czech Republic, Holland, Denmark, Germany, Hungary, Italy, Ireland, Portugal, The Netherlands, Russia, Canada, South Africa, Australia, New Zealand and even China.

Theme Park Tickets Direct: (www.themeparkticketsdirect.com) A specialist broker for attraction and theme park tickets in Florida, California, New York, Las Vegas and Disneyland Paris.

A quick check of the main tourist boards for your destination should also reveal a range of activities and attractions you might like to book or at least plan for. Once again, if you revert to your trusty search engine, you will find a wealth of information to help ensure you get the most out of your trip by being prepared in advance.

Passports and visas

For all foreign travel, you must hold a full ten-year passport, even for a day trip. If you don't currently hold a passport, you need to apply in good time (usually at least two months in advance).

You can get all the necessary advice from the Home Office website, **www.passport.gov.uk**, or call on 0870 521 0410 (lines are open 24 hours a day).

Some countries have a requirement for a passport to remain valid for a minimum period (up to six months) beyond the date of entry to that country, so check your passport is in good condition and valid for that extra period at the date of your return.

You also need to find out if you need a visa for your chosen destination, and there is an excellent online company which can do all this for you.

The Visa Company is the UK's largest visa and passport agency, handling visa requests and arranging all the necessary documentation for you. They organise and check all the paperwork, submit your passport and visa application, and collect and double-check the visa before sending it back to you.

They also have excellent up-to-the-minute passport and visa advice, with details of all the embassies you might need to contact and how long the process usually takes.

It is a complete one-stop shop for visa requirements, and you can even check in advance whether you need a visa and what the requirements are.

- Go to their home page by typing www.thevisacompany.com into your web browser.

- Use the drop-down menus to enter your nationality (it actually gives a list of countries), destination and the purpose of your trip (tourist).

- Press the **Go** button.

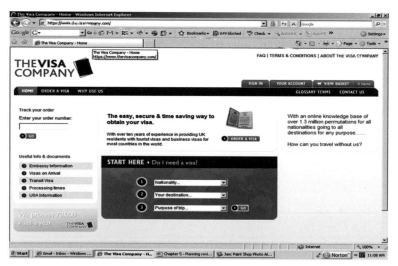

- The result will immediately show if you require a visa, and you can then decide if you would like to register with the Visa Company to handle the process for you.

However, some visas (notably for the USA) require you to appear in person, and you will need to make your own arrangements to visit the embassy in question.

You can also check the government website, **www.fco.gov.uk**, for details of foreign embassies.

- Click on **Travel Advice** and then scroll down the long menu on the left and click on the **Passports & Visas** link.

- Scroll down through the Passports and Visas text, and click on the **Consulate or Embassy** link (in blue) in the middle of the section.

- This brings up the full alphabetical list of foreign embassies in the UK and you can then select the country of your choice for visitor information.

- Click on the country you are interested in and full details of their UK embassy will come up.

- Click on their embassy **website** link and they will have a Visa section indicating all the requirements you need to meet if you need a visa to visit that country.

Creating a holiday worksheet

Making a good holiday plan is the key to a successful trip, and you can enhance this process by putting together your own worksheet of travel details. It doesn't need to be terribly complicated as long as you cover the essentials. To create a simple Word document with the necessary columns and rows, follow this process:

- Create a new document and put a title at the top.

- For the first table, position your cursor where you want it in the document.

- From the main Toolbar menu, click on **Table**.

- Click **Insert**.

- Click **Table** and a window will open up.

- Choose the number of columns and rows you want (2 and 10 in this example).

- Click **OK**.

- The table will appear in your document.

- To put text into the table, simply click in a box and start typing. The box will grow as you add text.

- If you need to add rows or columns, position your cursor in the table.

- Go back to **Table**.

- Click **Insert**.

- Click either **Columns to the Left/Right** or **Rows Above/Below**.

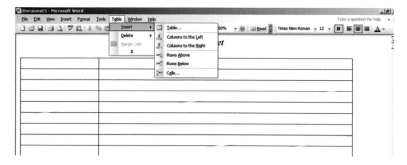

- Use the **Tab** key to move from box to box, or simply click in the box you want using your mouse.

- To adjust the width of each column, position your cursor over the vertical line and click and drag the column to the desired width.

- Once you have filled in your details for the first part, create a new sub-heading and insert the second table (3 columns and 5 rows).

- Repeat the process for the remaining sections of the worksheet.

Don't worry **if word processing is a struggle**

There is another excellent book in this series entitled *Silver Surfers' Colour Guide to Word Processing* by Wendy Hobson, which explains how to deal with this and many other word-processing topics.

If you have Microsoft Excel (as opposed to Word, which is the basic word processing program) it will make producing your own worksheet even easier. If all else fails, pen and paper still works!

Here is an example which you can adapt for your own usage. The first part is your travel checklist to keep close by while you are researching and booking. The second part is your factfile of essential information to take on holiday with you.

Holiday worksheet

PART ONE
Requirements checklist

Destination	
Budget	
Duration	
Number of passengers	
Transport	
Secondary transport	
Restrictions (direct flights, mobility issues, etc)	
Car hire	
Accommodation	
Transfers	

Research checklist

Destination	Tourist board	
	Independent site	
	Discussion forum	
	Others	
Transport	Airlines	
	Airport	
	Cruise lines	
	Rail	
Road routes	Ferries	
	Bus/coach	
Accommodation	Website	
	Trip advisor	
	Other reviews	
Car hire	At airport	
	At resort	
Transfers	By shuttle	
	By taxi	
	By limo	
	By bus/coach	

Costs checklist

	Estimate 1	Estimate 2	Estimate 3
Airfare	£	£	£
Airport parking	£	£	£
Airport transfers	£	£	£
Car hire	£	£	£
Hotel	£	£	£
Dining	£	£	£
Entertainment	£	£	£
Petrol	£	£	£
Souvenirs	£	£	£
Tips (notably for USA and cruises)	£	£	£
Miscellaneous:			
	£	£	£
	£	£	£
	£	£	£
	£	£	£
Total	£	£	£

Things to do checklist

Sightseeing	
Excursions	
Shows	
Restaurants	

Before departure

Confirm airline reservation	
Check baggage allowance	
Check hand luggage restrictions	
Confirm hotel reservation	
Confirm car hire reservation	
Confirm travel insurance for duration of trip	
Check passport validity (mustn't expire for 3 months after return)	
Check for any visa requirements	
Check for any vaccinations for overseas trips	
Leave your contact details with family/friend/neighbour	
Remember extra batteries for camera, etc	
Remember mobile phone charger	
Put name labels and destination address on luggage (but **not** home address)	
Ensure full supply of any medication	
Stop newspaper delivery	
Water plants	
Turn thermostat/water heater down	
Set light timers	
Empty household rubbish bins	
Unplug TV, computer and other electrical items	

For a car journey

Check tyre pressure, oil, coolant, windscreen washer fluid	
Check spare tyre pressure and car jack	
Print full directions	
Pack first aid kit	
Check breakdown cover (RAC, AA, etc.)	
Take necessary documentation for driving abroad	
Take driving licence and copy of car insurance policy	

PART TWO
Details to take with you

Trip dates:	
Flight number:	
Flight confirmation number:	
Accommodation confirmation number:	
Car rental confirmation number:	
Accommodation:	
Phone number:	
Address:	
E-mail:	
Fax number:	
Special dietary requests for flight:	
Special room requests for accommodation:	

Important document details

Passport numbers:	
Traveller's cheque numbers:	
Your doctor's details, name and phone number:	
Report lost traveller's cheques:	
Report lost credit cards:	
Important phone numbers:	
Addresses for postcards:	

Your reminder box

- Plan your holiday *before* you go online.

- Research your destination *before* booking anything.

- Establish whether you want a package holiday or a DIY booking.

- Carefully review all the dates, terms and conditions *before* clicking **Confirm** on your booking.

- Practice using the search engines and build up a list of trusted sites in your Favorites list.

Chapter 5
Understanding Travel Websites

Once you have established your holiday plan and worked out exactly what you are looking for, you need an understanding of the different types of websites that are available to you and, more importantly, what they can do for you.

Travel agents

Unlike pre-cyberspace days, when it was fairly obvious who your local travel agent was and what they offered, the modern online agent is a less straightforward creature.

The old 'big four' have changed with the times: Lunn Poly has become **www.thomson.co.uk**; Going Places is now **www.my travel.com**; Thomas Cook features as **www.thomascook.com** and First Choice holidays has an online presence as **www.firstchoice.co.uk**.

However, the bottom line is that although they are all officially online travel agents you are not necessarily getting the most comprehensive choice from them as they still primarily sell their own in-house brands.

The new breed

The new breed of online agents is slightly different as they do feature a much broader range of brands (contracted companies) for a wider variety of travel choice. Even so, they do not necessarily carry all airlines, hotels or car hire agencies.

Examples of the more comprehensive online agents are:

- **www.airline-network.co.uk**

- www.ebookers.com

- www.expedia.co.uk (the British arm of Expedia.com)

- www.flightcentre.co.uk

- www.lastminute.com

- www.opodo.co.uk

- www.trailfinders.com

- www.travelbag.co.uk

- www.travelcare.co.uk

- www.travelocity.co.uk

- www.travelrepublic.co.uk

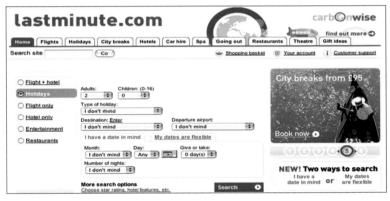

Advantages: A one-stop shop for all your travel needs, from packages to individual flights, hotels, car hire, airport parking and even travel insurance.

Disadvantages: Some online travel agents work on a commission basis with specific operators, hence they will promote only certain holiday brands or flights. The likes of MyTravel, Thomson, Thomas Cook and First Choice also tend to sell only the brands within their own group. You can sometimes get better prices going direct to the tour operator, airline or hotel.

Tour operators

Prior to the internet, there were few opportunities to book direct with the tour operators – the companies who actually organise most package holidays and charter flights. Now, however, you can deal directly with them, as well as via the travel agents.

Booking direct with a tour operator means you will usually get the best price *with that operator*. However, unlike a travel agent, you are searching only one source at a time, and you are not getting the much wider choice that most agents offer.

Here are some of the leading tour operator websites:

* www.airtours.co.uk
* www.cosmos.co.uk
* www.firstchoice.co.uk
* www.tcsignature.co.uk
* www.thomascook.co.uk
* www.thomson.co.uk
* www.titantravel.co.uk
* www.virginholidays.com
* www.xl.com

Don't worry about who it is

Ultimately, you don't need to work out whether you are booking with a tour operator, travel agent or Uncle Tom Cobley. As long as it is a reputable firm (see our advice in Chapter 8 on Buying Safely) and your booking is secure, the 'who it is' is far less important than 'what it is'. For a quick look at how the many different tour operators rate, you can also look up **www.reviewcentre.com**.

One very useful site for a wide range of independent tour operators is that of AITO – the Association of Independent Tour Operators. You will find a huge array of smaller-scale and specialist companies at **www.aito.co.uk**.

As a final thought on tour operators, it is always worth doing a search for a specialist if you have a particular type of holiday in mind, for example, walking holidays in the Peak District.

Advantages: Booking direct with the holiday vendor often ensures the best price and gives you a direct contact for any queries, etc. They specialise in package holidays, hence are a good place to look if you are not keen on the DIY approach of sorting out your own flights, accommodation, car hire, etc.

Disadvantages: You get a much narrower sample of holiday choice and may need to search multiple sites to get a good cross-section, while there is often little opportunity to take the DIY route, which can be cheaper.

Aggregators

It is worth noting the following group of companies as they can save you time on a variety of holiday/travel searches.

They are known in the travel business as aggregators (or comparator websites) as they simply compare products from a wide variety of agents and tour operators.

The big difference between an aggregator and a travel agent is that you do not make your purchase on the aggregator's website. Instead, you will be redirected to the website for the company selling the holiday/flight/car hire to make the booking.

Aggregators work on a commission basis with the companies they represent, which sometimes means they will not display the full range of options but rather a range that guarantees them a commission at the end of your search. This isn't always the case though and they are a good place to start, especially for things like flights and car hire.

TravelSupermarket

With TravelSupermarket you can search for Flights, Holidays, Hotels and Car Hire all at the touch of the various buttons. They are possibly the best of the bunch, with fast, accurate search criteria, useful additional features like Bargain Hunter (highlighting the cheapest flight searches in the previous three days) and general destination information. This is a good site to use if you are looking to book all the elements of a DIY holiday. Unlike some sites, all prices are for real-time searches, so you can be sure a better price hasn't come up while you are searching.

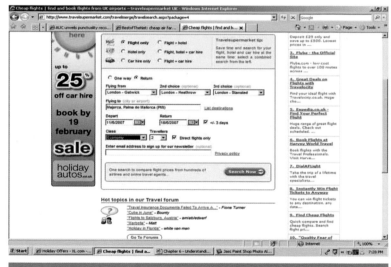

Kelkoo

Kelkoo is another big UK-based aggregator. Their speciality is searching and comparing a huge variety of products, hence you need to be more specific when searching.

Their special travel features include a Trip Planner section, which can compile a range of short break trips, combining flights with hotel and car hire, and an Experiences section, which offers some novel experiences like rally driving and biplane flights. However, their package holiday choice is extremely limited.

Kayak

A third major aggregator is the new UK site for the big American company Kayak, hence you need to be sure to type in www.kayak.co.uk (not www.kayak.com, where all prices will be in US dollars). Some results (notably for hotels) also connect to US sites like Orbitz, which also show prices in dollars.

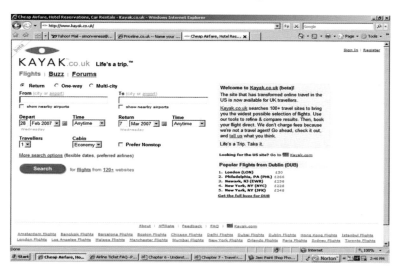

In addition to flight searches, Kayak offers a Buzz section which highlights popular trip ideas and the cheapest results for recent searches, and a Forums section – although this latter is heavily biased towards American travellers and you can find better information elsewhere.

Their Flight search, though, is one of the best as it offers a variety of different criteria – by cheapest price, airline, non-stop (1 stop or 2+ stops), specific departure times, multiple departure points and even a price range. It also has search Tips and a handy Best Fare Trend feature, which shows an average flight price over the previous 90 days.

SideStep

Another American company recently launched in the UK is SideStep, which is useful for flights, hotels, package holidays, car hire and a good range of other activities. They also have their own online travel guides for many destinations (provided by Frommer's, so not necessarily 100 per cent up to date).

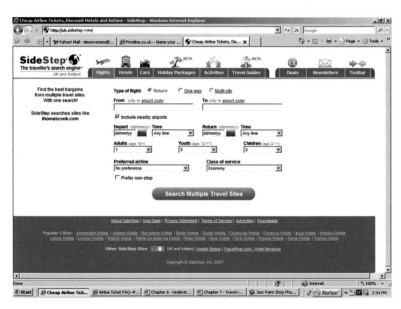

However, their package holiday options are poor as they don't search many tour operator websites while, for hotels, you need to know the *airport* that serves destinations like Majorca/ Mallorca (Palma de Mallorca) and the Costa Blanca (Alicante).

More aggregator links:

• **www.carrentals.co.uk** Searches all the major car hire sites.

• **www.cheapflights.co.uk** Well-established UK site that provides search results in date order.

• **www.comparethemarket.com** Travel insurance.

Advantages: The ability to search multiple sites quickly and get the cheapest fare in most instances. They can save time and provide useful extras, like 'bargain hunter' and 'popular search' features. Great for flights, hotels and car hire.

Disadvantages: They still miss some sites – like charter airlines and tour operators   and you must scrutinise their search results carefully for things that don't meet your criteria. Not so good for package holidays. They can also display non-valid fares at times.

Bidding websites

The final category of websites are the bidding sites which allow you to name your own price for things like hotels and flights. The big incentive is you can save significantly on price, but the sites are a lot more complicated (and limiting, in many cases).

These are really only for when you are fully confident in your internet use, have plenty of time to study the terms and conditions involved and can be flexible with your travel requirements.

Before using a bidding site, you should check the other websites to get an idea of the lowest price available and read the terms and conditions of your bid *extremely* carefully before taking the plunge.

Priceline

The UK version of this big American site is the prime example of a bidding website. It works in two ways:

- As a straightforward agent, listing a variety of flight, hotel, city break and car hire deals. Their hotels also come with a handy Reviews feature, where recent guests have made their comments and given the hotel a rating.

- And with their 'Name your own price' section, where you get to put forward your own price or bid for a hotel or flight.

However, with this latter process, you do not know in advance exactly what you are bidding for, and you must pay for it *before* your bid is even accepted. If it is rejected, there are also restrictions on how soon you may bid again for a similar hotel or flight.

For hotels, you can only bid for an area of a city and the star rating of the hotel, not a specific hotel. Priceline's idea of a 3 or 4-star hotel may also not be the same as another agent's.

For flights, you can bid only for a specific date, not a time, hence you may end up with an early-morning or late-night flight, or a return that gets back overnight. For short breaks it is simply not worth it, as you may end up with a very late flight followed by an early-morning return.

If you are keen to learn more about the likes of Priceline, we recommend the website **www.biddingfortravel.com** for more help and advice.

Advantages: They can sometimes yield major savings and are particularly useful when regular fares are high.

Disadvantages: They don't have the same range of products as other websites and there are more restrictions on their flights and hotel results. There is no option to get Multi-city (or 'open-jaw' flights) and they can involve flight timings that may not be convenient and hotels in locations you might not choose yourself. No good for last-minute trips. Reservations cannot be cancelled, transferred, changed or refunded.

Your reminder box

- Travel agents offer one-stop shopping, but may not cover every option.

- Tour operators are strong in package sales but sell only their in-house brands.

- Aggregators check a wide variety of sellers but are not the best option for package sales.

- Bidding sites may result in large savings, but beware the risks involved in not knowing what you are getting until after you've paid for it.

- Check more than one source to be sure you have the full range of what's available.

Chapter 6

Understanding the Travel Essentials

Once you have established your holiday plan and understand how the different websites work, the next step is to acquaint yourself with the various online booking options.

The nuts and bolts of the travel world vary from the obvious to the fiendishly intricate, and many of them revolve around that all-important factor – price.

Is the price right?

Knowing you've got a fair price is one of the most important things in booking online, and there are several things you can do to help ensure peace of mind (also see Chapter 8, Buying Safely).

As a general rule, the earlier you book the better price you will get (especially with the low-cost airlines), but some companies – notably tour operators and even some cruise lines – do reduce prices nearer the departure date if they have spare capacity.

There are several other ways to get the cheapest rate:

• Travel in midweek rather than at weekends.

• Be flexible with your travel dates. If you can give a range of dates when searching for a flight or hotel, it may well reveal something cheaper than if you just provide a specific date.

• Avoid the school holidays (use government website **www.direct.gov.uk**: click on **Education and learning**; then **Schools**; scroll down and click on **School life**; then **Term dates and school holidays**, and click on the **Find out term dates** link; this opens a new window where you can enter your postcode or Local Authority and see all the local school term times).

• Look for off-peak times at bigger destinations by seeing how prices vary from month to month; the autumn and early spring typically see lower prices throughout Europe, while the UK summer is a good off-peak time to visit southern Africa and the Caribbean.

• Go at the last minute. All the travel agent websites advertise late deals or you can just try a quick search using the criteria "UK last-minute travel deals".

• Look for Fare Alerts on many websites. These offer to search prices on a regular basis and send you an e-mail alert if your desired price comes up.

In many instances, it helps just to know what the basic, standard price is for a particular flight or holiday package. And you can usually find this out quickly and easily by searching any of the main travel agent websites.

• Type www.expedia.co.uk in the Address bar.

- If, say, you want a rough idea of flight prices for a weekend trip to Paris, click on the **Flights** tab and input those details.

- Click **Search**.
- The results will immediately give you a range of prices with four or five airlines, flying non-stop or with one stop.

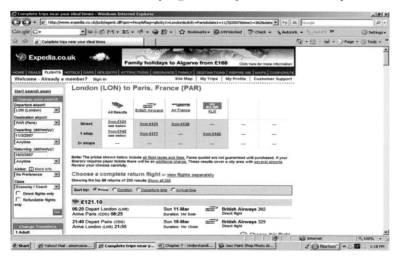

Don't worry about which sites you use

With practice, you will develop your own favourite sites to search. It doesn't really matter whether you use Expedia, LastMinute, Travelcare, TravelSupermarket, Priceline or someone else. As long as you follow the essential principle of getting a range of quotes from the different sites, you can be confident you have a good idea of the right price to pay.

Once you have a rough idea of the price, you can be more serious in your flight booking (see Chapter 11).

When you understand how each element of holiday travel works, you can be sure you have all the facts at your fingertips when it comes to making the final decision.

Understanding package holidays

Package holidays are just that – a package which includes the basic elements of travel: accommodation, transport (either flights or coach), transfers (or car hire), meals (unless specified) and, sometimes, attraction tickets.

Booking a package has the benefit of involving far less work than booking each element separately. The drawback is that you may not get the best possible price and you are stuck with the tour operator's travel timings and hotel choice.

Virtually all the big tour operators and travel agents make the booking process straightforward. Don't feel rushed into making your choice – the important thing is to take your time and read the details carefully.

We will show you how to put this into practice in Chapter 10.

Good words to know

All inclusive: Full board and drinks all included. May also include things like water sports and other activities.

Bed and breakfast (or B&B): Accommodation plus breakfast (full breakfast in the UK; a continental-style breakfast in Europe and the US, unless otherwise stated).

European plan: Hotel rate that does not include meals.

Full board: Breakfast, lunch and dinner all included.

Half board: Breakfast and dinner both included, but not lunch.

Room only: Accommodation only, no meals provided.

Self catering: Kitchen facilities but no meals provided.

Good words to know

Off season (or low season): A resort or destination's quietest period. Prices may be lower during this time.

Peak season (or high season): Busiest season or seasons of the year, usually the main school holidays and half-terms. Rates are usually highest during this time.

Requests (or special requests): Some online booking engines will allow you to specify certain room requests, such as non-smoking, first floor or early check-in. Requests are not guaranteed but are taken into consideration when your room is assigned.

Shoulder season: Period of time between peak and off season, when rates are somewhat lower and crowds somewhat lighter.

Understanding flights

If your travel requirements are limited to just a flight, the booking process and terms involved are somewhat simpler.

You have a choice of either booking directly on the airline's own website or using Expedia, Travelocity or other booking sites.

Good words to know

Charter airlines: Airlines that are hired (often by tour operators) to carry passengers purely between set destinations. You may see longer delays among the charter airlines.

Checked luggage: Suitcases and other luggage that goes in the plane's hold when you check in.

Low-cost airlines: Specialise in cheap, short-haul routes, with minimal frills and 'pay as you go' service.

'Open-jaw' (or 'multi-city') flight: Lets you fly to one city or airport and return from another. For example, flying from London to New York but returning to London from Washington. All scheduled airlines should be able to cater for 'open-jaw' flights, whereas charter airlines cannot.

Scheduled airlines: Airlines that maintain regular services between all the main airports. These tend to have the best reliability records.

In our experience, it is best to check prices on both – and get at least three quotes – to establish the range of prices before you book. Sometimes an airline's own website has the best price, sometimes not.

The aggregator websites are also particularly good at searching for flights, so be sure to try at least one from: **TravelSupermarket.com, Kelkoo.co.uk, TravelJungle.co.uk** and **SkyScanner.net** (the latter two of which specialise in low-cost airlines).

The important things to remember for booking a flight are:

• Your travel dates. You must enter specific dates to start with, but some sites let you search by + or – seven days.

• The number of people in your party. Some airlines offer lower rates for seniors, but most charge the full adult rate.

• Your exact destination. New York has three major airports, for example, while Chicago has two (London officially has five – Heathrow, Gatwick, Luton, Stansted and London City). If you can be flexible with the destination airport, enter 'New York any' or 'Paris any'.

• Always double-check the results that come up when you do an online search to make sure they have the right dates and destinations.

Being flexible with your dates pays biggest dividends here. If you go directly to a major airline like British Airways, it will show you how the price can vary according to different days of the week.

• Go to the BA website by typing www.ba.com into your web browser.

- Make sure you enter their UK site rather than the US site on their home page.

- Enter your flight requirements for a specific date (say, for a flight to New York).

- Click **Get Flights**.

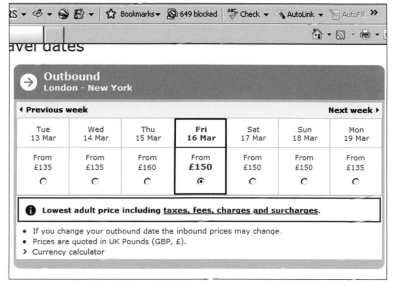

- See how the price peaks over the weekend? If you choose a midweek date a few days earlier, you would save £15 per person on each leg of the flight.

Look out for sneaky new 'extras' that some airlines have introduced, including having to pay for checked luggage and a boarding fee if you want to be among the first on the plane (on some low-cost airlines).

Passengers on all flights from the UK also have to pay Air Passenger Duty (or APD) per person, which is basically a government tax. This should be included among all the taxes, fees and surcharges in the price.

Beware sites that *do not* include all the taxes and other extras in their bottom line. It is easy to think you have found a cheaper flight only to reach the payment stage and find they *then* add on all the surcharges and the price suddenly jumps by £100 or more.

Also, look out for sites that don't put the cheapest option at the top of their results selection. Some have Sponsored Links, which means they promote certain airlines first, and you may need to scroll down through the results to find the cheapest.

Pay special attention

Study the terms and conditions for your flight before completing the booking. Some cheaper alternatives do not allow you any leeway for changing details without a hefty fee.

We will put these lessons into practice in Chapter 11.

Understanding accommodation

There is a vast choice of accommodation these days, but hotels remain the top option for the majority. And, once again, they require more details when you do it yourself.

Don't overlook the possibilities of other types of accommodation including apartments, villas and gîtes (in France – village-style homes where you stay as part of the family). See Chapter 12 for more novel ideas.

Understanding hotels

Previously, when you booked a hotel through your travel agent, you simply booked a room for the dates and resort of your choice. You were assigned a standard room and never thought anything else of it.

Online, you must be aware of other criteria:

- Hotel class: Most booking sites and hotels operate a rating system (1–5 stars or A ratings). Virgin Holidays use V ratings, just to be different. The price, facilities, service and quality obviously increase with the rating.

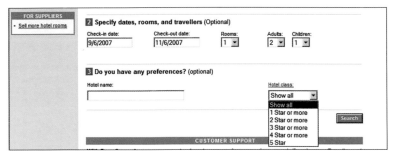

- Room type: Is it a twin (two single beds, for two people), double (a double bed), queen, king, triple (for three people) or quad (for four)? Some rooms will even have added amenities like a jacuzzi or whirlpool tub, or kitchen facilities.

- Price basis: Room only, bed and breakfast, half-board or full board. Most hotels sell on a room-only basis, unless specified.

- Special requests: Smoking/non-smoking, connecting rooms, special view (sea, lake, etc.), near a lift ('elevator' in American hotels), ground floor only (first floor in the US), disabled access.

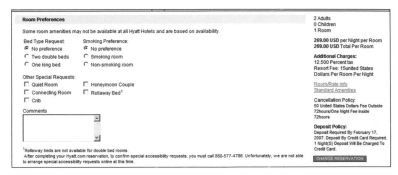

- Facilities: In-room tea/coffee-making facilities, fridge/microwave, swimming pool, restaurant, bar, internet access, business facilities, fitness facilities, air conditioning, parking, room service, spa facilities, laundry, pets allowed.

• What is nearby: Shops, cinemas, restaurants, a main road, etc. Most sites should give you some idea of this and a hotel's own website should have a more detailed description of its location, with a map and driving directions.

Don't worry about room types

If all the different possibilities for room type and facilities leave you bewildered, it is still possible to choose a standard room and ignore all the upgrades, additions, etc. You can still request some of these extras when you check in, although it pays to know in advance what might be available.

There are also several relatively new categories of hotel-type accommodation which you may encounter.

• A Suites hotel has rooms with a separate bedroom and living-room area, usually with basic kitchen facilities (fridge, microwave and/or cooker). They are typically more spacious than a standard hotel room and work better for longer stays and a home-from-home base.

- An 'efficiency' is a room with basic kitchen facilities.

- Condo-hotels are an American innovation, combining hotel facilities with apartment-type ownership, managed primarily as hotels.

- Apart-hotels are serviced apartments for short-term rental, but usually for longer than a typical hotel stay.

- Formule 1 is a French brand which has now gone worldwide and consists of the most basic type of accommodation – usually just a room with a bed, TV and WC/wash basin (sometimes a shower).

Pay special attention

While the star rating system is widely used in Europe, there is no standardised equivalent in the USA. Hotels still get a star rating on most websites but this is *not* an official rating, only a general guide.

Understanding apartments and villas

Apartments and holiday homes (villas or vacation homes) use slightly different booking criteria, as well as different search terms (see Chapter 12).

There is no established rating system for villas, so you need to be more inquisitive about quality. Some companies use the term 'executive' or 'luxury' but they should also detail what makes an executive home (usually a higher grade of facility, with pool, TVs, linens, furnishings, etc, rather than a bigger property).

You will need to check the following criteria:

- The number of bedrooms.

- The exact location. They can be either individual houses or part of a resort community with large numbers of similar properties nearby.

- What deposit is required.

- Whether they supply the keys (or a security code) for direct entry or if you need to collect the keys from a separate office.

- What regular cleaning services are offered.

- Where is the nearest supermarket for groceries.

- Is there a local contact if anything goes wrong with the property.

Don't worry about villa rental

This is one of the fastest-growing accommodation types in the world, especially in America, and often represents a major saving for large family groups staying together. Many people approach villa rental reluctantly but soon find it suits them far better than staying in a hotel, especially as it can be more restful.

One of the big advantages of renting a villa is that you can usually check it out online, often in some detail. Most sites include a photo library of each villa while some even provide video.

Understanding car hire

When you start to book DIY holidays and travel, car hire quickly becomes an important component of the booking process if you want to be able to get around easily.

The first thing to establish is whether or not you need a car in the first place. In big cities like Paris, San Francisco, New York, Berlin and Amsterdam it is easy to get around by public transport and on foot. The only thing you should check in advance is the transport options from the airport to your accommodation.

If you decide you do need a car and are happy to drive on the 'wrong' side of the road (as is the case with most of the rest of the world), you should consider the following criteria:

- For holiday purposes, you can usually go a size smaller than the car you drive at home.

- Check the boot size (or the 'trunk' in US terms). Make sure you will be able to fit all your luggage in.

- Your own insurance probably won't cover driving a hire car abroad, hence it is vital to purchase comprehensive coverage. At the very least you will need: Collision Damage Waiver (or Damage Liability Waiver), which covers any damage to or loss of the vehicle; and Supplementary Liability Insurance (or Extended Protection), which covers third party liability and uninsured motorist protection.

- Check whether your travel/health insurance covers you for Personal Accident (for anyone in your vehicle who incurs medical expenses as the result of an accident) and Personal Effects (for theft of or damage to personal items inside the hire car).

- Local rates, taxes and fees can easily add up if you leave car hire until you arrive, but most companies now offer all-inclusive rates in advance, which can save you money. Make sure you take a credit card when you collect the car, as many companies refuse cash deposits.

- Check if you need automatic or manual – most cars in the USA are automatic but you may find only manuals in some parts of Europe.

- Check the policy on fuel – the best option is always to top the fuel tank up before you return it rather than paying the hire company's enormous refuelling rate.

- Remember your driving licence – both the card and the paper part if you have the newer version. The hire company will need to check both before you can drive off.

Midsize Car

⊖ Hide car image, make/model, and capacity for each car.

	Car Hire Company	Doors	Location	Total Price	
	Alamo		🚗	£122.26	Select
	Pontiac G6 sedan or similar, 2 adult(s), 3 child(ren), 2 large suitcase(s), 2 carry-on(s).				
	Alamo		🚗	£131.15	Select
	Oldsmobile Alero or similar, 4 adult(s), luggage capacity not available.				
	National		🚗	£132.10	Select
	Pontiac G6 sedan or similar, 5 adult(s), 4 large suitcase(s).				

Don't worry about different car insurances

Most companies offer fully comprehensive policies if you book in advance, and they can often represent a saving on buying it when you arrive. Look up **www.alamo.co.uk/brits** for US car hire as a good example.

Understanding rail travel

Unravelling the vagaries of the various rail networks just in Great Britain could be a book in itself, let alone the considerations once you venture into Europe!

Thankfully, there are some excellent online resources for sorting out and booking your rail travel, and this is just another area where you can really make the internet work for you to simplify a complicated system.

Your basic requirements for rail travel are easy to follow:

- For information on rail travel within the UK, consult **www.rail.co.uk** or **www.thetrainline.co.uk**.

- Book in advance wherever possible (you can only book up to 3 months in advance in the UK and Europe).

- Travel off peak and be flexible for the best fares.

- For European rail travel, consult **www.raileurope.co.uk**.

- For journeys further afield and more exotic routes, look up **www.greatrail.com**.

One other site you should bookmark for advice – and inspiration – is **www.seat61.com**, set up by British rail specialist Mark Smith to encourage people to undertake more travel by rail and actually enjoy their journey, as opposed to just jumping on a plane.

We will put these elements into practice in Chapter 11.

Understanding ferries and cruises

Ferries and cruises are more complicated and require more careful consideration, although that shouldn't stop you seeking out the great value and bargains to be had here as well.

The main requirement is to take more time over your research. There are some fabulous websites for background reading, and you should start here before making a booking.

The UK's Passenger Shipping Association is at the forefront of providing invaluable independent advice. Look up their website at **www.discover-cruises.co.uk**.

Understanding ferry travel

The principal requirements for ferry travel are similar to those for rail. Therefore the things to bear in mind are:

• Book as far in advance as possible for the best fares.

• Most ferry companies offer discounts for booking online.

- Have all your personal details to hand when booking, including things like passport numbers, make, registration number and length of car.

- Keep a careful note of your booking confirmation.

- Book a sailing time that you can make without having to dash, but don't panic if you miss it, as there's usually room on the next sailing. If you're early, you may be able to go on an earlier departure.

- For an at-a-glance guide to ferries and all the possible routes (and to book), look up **www.seaview.co.uk/ferries.asp**.

Understanding cruise travel

Taking a cruise is one of the great holiday choices nowadays, but you must decide your requirements in advance. There is something for everyone in the wide world of cruising, but you must first look at:

- *Where* you want to go – there are cruises virtually everywhere, but the Mediterranean, Caribbean, Alaska, Northern Europe and the Canaries remain the main choices.

However, if you want something really novel, there are voyages to the Chilean fjords, Antarctica, Greenland, the Far East and South Pacific.

- *When* you want to go – most areas have a season (although the Caribbean is year-round), hence Alaskan cruises run May–September, in the Mediterranean it's April–November, in Northern Europe June–August and in the Canaries November–April.

- The *size of ship* you want – there are small ships with only a handful of people aboard and glittering mega-liners with 3,000 passengers. The latter have far more facilities and entertainment but are more impersonal.

- The *style of cruise*, whether formal or informal – there are ships where you still need to dress up for dinner and those where you can be entirely casual.

- The *type of cabin* you need – there are numerous categories, and you will be asked if you want an inside cabin (without a view) or an outside one (with a window or porthole); a cabin with a balcony; a suite or penthouse; and even what deck you want to be on (the higher up in the ship, the better the view, but the higher the price).

• And the *nationality* of your crew – many cruise lines are predominantly American, but there are also mainly British lines, some that are Italian, German or Spanish.

You can also consult several independent magazines on the subject, such as **www.worldofcruisingmagazine.com**, which has an extensive Cruise Planner section, as well as an online edition feature (we should say that Simon is the editor!).

Once again, there is a huge amount of information on the net, and your favourite search engine can be your best friend. CruiseCritic.com is another good source of information, although it is primarily geared to American cruisers.

We will put these lessons into practice in Chapter 11.

Currency conversion

As a final thought on price and monetary concerns, you might find that you get some quotes in different currencies. Visit currency exchange website **www.oanda.com** and use their Quick Converter at the top of the page to change all prices into the one you need.

For example, changing Euros into pounds:

• Click on the black down arrow to open a drop-down menu.

• Click on the required currency.

• Click on **Convert**.

Oanda will give you the day's exchange rate and a box for entering the amount you want to convert.

• Type in the figure you want to convert from Euros into pounds.

• Click on **New Conversion** and the answer will appear.

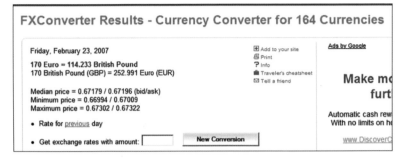

FXConverter Results - Currency Converter for 164 Currencies

Friday, February 23, 2007

170 Euro = 114.233 British Pound
170 British Pound (GBP) = 252.991 Euro (EUR)

Median price = 0.67179 / 0.67196 (bid/ask)
Minimum price = 0.66994 / 0.67009
Maximum price = 0.67302 / 0.67322

• Rate for previous day

• Get exchange rates with amount: [____]   **New Conversion**

⊞ Add to your site
🖨 Print
❓ Info
🧳 Traveler's cheatsheet
✉ Tell a friend

Ads by Google

Make mo
furt

Automatic cash rew
With no limits on h

www.DiscoverC

Your reminder box

• Become familiar with basic travel terminology.

• Learn the difference between booking flights with a specific airline and using an online agent.

• Take into account the extra considerations when booking accommodation, especially the room types.

• Consider apartments and villas as an alternative to hotels.

• Work out if you need car hire and be familiar with the booking process.

• Use the four main websites to help with rail travel.

• For sea travel, make sure you do your homework before you book anything.

Chapter 7
Specialist Travel

In addition to the many regular packages and travel options available to you, there is a huge range of alternative opportunities, from adventure holidays and disabled-accessible travel to educational activities and trips for single travellers.

Gourmet cooking, painting courses, pottery classes and even learning Qigong on a Greek island are all on the modern menu. You just need to take your pick!

Adventure holidays

Taking a holiday that's on the more adventurous side is one of the fastest-growing trends in travel, and you can try your hand at almost anything, from cattle-ranching to white-water rafting.

There are 'soft' adventure options, where there is little actual physical challenge, and 'hard' options, where you need to be pretty fit to tackle many of the activities. There are also plenty that cater for seniors and those with disabilities.

Some tour operators have even built whole new programmes around more activity-orientated pursuits, like Crystal Holidays, who now have Crystal Active (**www.crystal-active.co.uk**).

The basics

Here is what you should do before booking:

- Check *exactly* what is involved, from the distances you may need to walk to any other physical activities, like horse-riding or climbing. Just because something is advertised as a 'soft' option, doesn't mean it won't have a physical component.

- Make sure you are fully covered by your travel insurance for all the activities involved.

- Try to ensure you will be travelling with people of your own age group and/or nationality.

- Talk to your doctor in advance about any health concerns involved and get a medical check-up if in any doubt.

- Check the company's policy in case of any medical emergencies.

The options

Adventure cruises: An increasingly attractive way to visit more unusual parts of the world like Antarctica, the North Cape and Arctic, the Galapagos Islands and Patagonia. With specialist lectures and organised excursions, they can cater for all but the seriously disabled.

Cycling: Britain, Spain and France are all popular for biking holidays of various kinds, while cruise lines Ocean Village and Island Cruises both carry bikes for cycling excursions at many ports of call.

Fishing: Scotland is a prime location for many types of angling, especially salmon and fly fishing, while Florida in the USA is a great source for both freshwater and offshore fishing.

Horse-riding: Simple trail-riding can be found throughout Europe, while more serious trekking is on offer in the USA, South America and South Africa. Visit America for a great selection of 'dude' ranches (cattle-ranching for beginners).

Motor sports: 4-wheel drive safaris are highly popular, as well as karting/quad-biking, military vehicle driving and even rallying. In America, you can try the 170mph motor speedways of the Richard Petty driving schools.

Walking: From the South Downs to the Andes in Peru, there is a fabulous range (no pun intended!) of walking and hiking holidays. But do make a point of checking how strenuous they are. The Andes are especially demanding.

Water sports: Kayaking, rafting and boating of all kinds can be found almost worldwide, with the Mediterranean and America being key destinations.

Winter sports: Skiing is now offered almost everywhere there is a hill and enough white stuff to get you sliding. The Alps remain the top draw, but the USA and Canada are a good alternative.

The directory

Once you have ascertained what you'd like to try, you are free to look at some wonderful possibilities. When it comes to your search terms, be specific about what you are looking for, e.g. "Walking holidays" France or "Ranching holidays" USA.

• To get you started, the directory **www.travel-quest.co.uk** lists dozens of opportunities.

• Search by Activity (main list) for things like Cycling and Walking.

• For Special Categories like groups, gap year and singles holidays look at the separate list down the right-hand side.

For practice, look for their **Equestrian/Horse** category on the main Activities list and click on the sub-heading **ranching**.

- This takes you to a list of possibilities for ranching holidays (look for the Union Jack symbol to indicate British-based or owned companies).

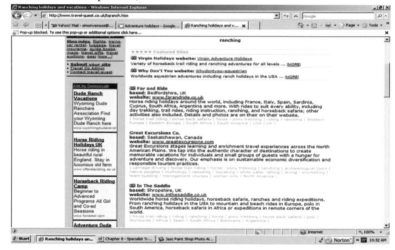

- Scroll down and click on the **web address** for one of them (e.g. Ranch America).

> **Ranch America**
> **based:** Hertfordshire, UK
> **website:** www.ranchamerica.co.uk
> An extensive choice of ranch and outdoor adventures which can be enjoyed by people of all ages.
> | ranching | riding | horse trail riding | horse drawn | white water rafting | USA | Canada |

- You will be taken to their site, and can look up all the holidays they offer.

Don't worry **about asking for information**

Most of these smaller, specialist companies are equipped to answer individual queries. Just click on the **Contact Us** link (often on the top right of a website or at the very bottom) and it will open an e-mail enquiry window. Type in your question, remember to add your e-mail contact details for a reply, and hit **Send** or **Submit**.

More information

General adventure holiday information can be found through:

- **www.activitiesabroad.com** Activities Abroad offer some excellent hiking, off-road adventures and kayaking.

- **www.inntravel.co.uk** Inntravel features walking, cycling, skiing and horse-riding.

- **www.travelsphere.co.uk** Travelsphere has an Active Holidays section.

- **www.virginholidays.co.uk** Virgin Holidays features an Adventure section.

- **www.whydontyou.com** Why Don't You has Sports & Pastimes pages.

Another valuable site is **In My Prime**, with travel and general lifestyle advice for the over 50s.

- Type www.inmyprime.co.uk in the Address bar.

- Click on the **lifestyle** link in the menu on the left-hand side.

- Scroll down to the foot of the page where there are links for Staying In, Going Out and Travel.

- Click on **Travel** for their excellent travel advice page.

- At the foot, you will find a Click here link for more suggestions.

> Click here to see our directory of organisations who can help.

- Click on the words **Click here** (in red) and it offers a wide range of thought-provoking and activity-orientated holidays.

More general links:

- www.adventurecompany.co.uk
- www.adventuretravel.about.com
- www.discover-the-world.co.uk
- www.nationalgeographic.com/adventure
- www.trekamerica.co.uk

Educational/creative holidays

When it comes to more unusual and creative pursuits, there is an almost endless stream of new and inviting opportunities.

Arts and crafts, culture, food and drink, gardening, history, wildlife, writing – virtually anything can be turned into a holiday. Much of it is also aimed at a senior audience, as the over 50s increasingly demand more from their holidays.

The options

Arts and crafts: From metalwork to jewellery-making and antiques to photography, there are a wealth of creative courses available in some wonderful places like Spain, France and the USA as well as Britain.

Food and drink: If you've ever wanted to learn a foreign cuisine or just indulge in a gourmet break somewhere, both are possible.

Health and well-being: Healthy and holistic lifestyles are a big new trend, hence you can find holidays offering yoga, pilates, meditation, spa treatments, fitness courses and much more, especially in India and the Far East.

Painting: Studying the masters or just learning the basics of watercolours, plus more elaborate subjects like printmaking and drawing skills can all be found, notably in Britain, France and Italy.

The directory

Once again, Travel Quest is your best friend for all things creative/educational.

- Type www.travel-quest.co.uk into the Address bar.

- Scroll down to the Special Interest Holidays heading.

- Click on a link like **Food & Drink** and enjoy browsing the nine categories that come up. With 18 different Special Interest sections, you have some wonderful options.

Don't worry **about trying your own searches**

If you have an interest you'd like to combine with a holiday, there may well be someone offering it. Just use your favourite search engine and type in something like Quilting holidays. If using the word 'holiday' reaps no rewards, try the American word 'vacation' instead, and you will find results relevant to the USA. Remember to check whether a company takes bookings from UK customers – that is not necessarily the case with *all* sites ending in **.com** (but sites ending in **.co.uk** *are* UK specific).

More information

Travel World also has a useful directory of offbeat ideas and hobbies, which lists the possibilities by tour operator (although they are not comprehensive).

* Type www.travel.world.co.uk into the Address bar.

* Scroll down to the Hobbies & Interests section.

- Click on categories that interest you (say **Health & Well-Being Holidays**).

- This will bring you to a directory of operators offering various varieties of health-orientated pursuits.

- Click on one of them (say **La Buissiere Yoga Retreat Centre**).

- This takes you to their contact details within the Travel World directory.

- Click on their **web address** (Uniform Resource Locator) and you will go to their home page.

More useful links:

* **www.destinationprovence.co.uk** Painting, cookery and wine appreciation.

* **www.frenchconnections.co.uk** 370 adventures throughout France.

* **www.ilcollegio.com** Art, gastronomy, Italian culture.

* **www.skyros.com** Well-being, writing courses, photography, dance and more.

* **www.whydontyou.com** Cookery, dance, photography and more.

Don't worry **about trying a small company**

Many of these companies are only small operators and will probably be new to you. Don't be afraid to check them out as you will find some real specialists. Just remember to check for some kind of bonding so your booking is secure. A full tour operator must have an ATOL licence while a travel agent should have an ABTA licence or some other form of insurance bonding (see also page 118).

Gap/extended holidays

The idea of a gap year is prevalent among young people – taking a year off to go travelling, to study something different or do volunteer work. However, the idea of 'Grey gappers' has caught on recently, with seniors also taking extended time away from home on something travel-related.

With the kids having left home, some people have a strong urge to spend up to a year abroad, either visiting new places or on a project of some kind. There is even a term for it – SKI-ing, or Spending the Kids' Inheritance!

You can go caravanning across America, polish up your golf skills, learn a new language or trade, take up water sports or volunteer with a non-governmental organisation in Ghana or Sri Lanka.

What you need to consider:

• Specialist insurance for an extended period away is essential.

• A full physical check-up before you leave.

• Background research – study the area you are considering visiting at length.

• Contacting someone who has done something similar – the websites below all offer useful case studies, message boards and contacts.

• Whether you are looking for a luxury experience or if you are ready to rough it.

• Learning some basic First Aid.

The website **www.goldengapyears.com** is an excellent source of information, ideas and feedback, but needless to say this is not something that should be entered into lightly.

Don't worry **about this newsletter**

Although we advise against signing up for travel company newsletters in general terms (they generate too much junk e-mail), the GoldenGapYears Newsletter is definitely worth subscribing to as it contains a lot of up-to-the-minute advice.

More useful links:

• www.gapyear.com

• www.gapyearsforgrownups.co.uk

• www.questoverseas.com/escapes

• www.singulartravel.co.uk

Holidays for the disabled

There are now numerous companies that offer disabled-accessible holidays, hotels and activities, as well as some excellent organisations providing support and advice.

So, if you have a hip problem, partial sight, MS, have had a stroke or are confined to a wheelchair but would still like to take a cruise or a package holiday, there is someone who can provide it for you.

In travel terms, America in general and Florida in particular are extremely mobility-friendly, while many major European resorts also cater well.

Don't worry **about the term 'handicapped'**

Americans tend to use 'handicapped' rather than 'disabled', and that is the term most US organisations are most comfortable with. They don't mean any offence by it, it is just a strange use of terminology from the British perspective; in the US, 'disabled' is the more pejorative term.

Finding disabled-friendly holidays

Use search terms such as "Disabled holidays" UK or "white water rafting" disabled for sites that include disabled facilities.

A good starting point is The Big Project travel directory.

• Type www.thebigproject.co.uk into the Address bar.

• Press **Enter**.

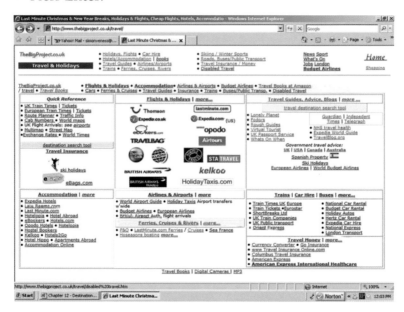

• Click on the **Disabled Travel** link near the top of the page.

• Browse the links under Specialist Holiday Companies.

Specialist Holiday Companies
• Access-travel.co.uk Holidays for disabled persons
• AccessibleTravel.co.uk Wide selection of accessible holidays
• Breakaway holidays and weekends For small groups and individuals with 24 hour support from experienced carers
• Sportability.org Provides sporting and adventurous activities for people with all forms of disability
• Disability Snowsport.org.uk Enabling those with a disability to ski alongside the able bodied as equals at all ski facilities and resorts
• Epic-Enabled.com Offers overland camping & adventure safari holidays in Southern Africa to the physically disabled traveller
• JST.org.uk Adventure sailing holidays for disabled people
• Radar.org.uk Royal Association for Disability and Rehabilitation - National UK organisation run by and for disabled people

Packages

There are a number of British tour operators who cater particularly well for customers with disabilities. These include:

- www.abletogo.com
- www.access-travel.co.uk
- www.barrheadtravel.co.uk
- www.canbedone.co.uk
- www.carewellholidays.com
- www.chalfont-line.co.uk
- www.disabilitytravel.co.uk

Specialities

For offbeat and adventurous holidays for people with disabilities, try some of the following:

- www.bendrigg.org.uk Activity courses for the disabled.
- www.brucetrust.org.uk Canal boating in the UK.
- www.disabilitysnowsport.org.uk Winter sports.
- www.globetrotterclub.com Educational, safaris and à la carte holidays.
- www.optionsholidays.co.uk Supported holidays worldwide for people with learning disabilities.
- www.staffordshiremoorlandsfarmholidays.co.uk Farm holidays.

Cruises

Only the most modern ships (from the late 1990s on) can genuinely offer facilities for the disabled, with extra-width doors to cabins, roll-in showers and ramps on to the decks. Older ships are not terribly wheelchair accessible.

Look for a cruise where the ship docks in port rather than having to use small boats (tenders) to go ashore. If you'd prefer not to fly, look for UK cruises from Southampton, Dover and Harwich. Some cruise lines will also accept the disabled only with an able-bodied companion (in case of emergency).

The Passenger Shipping Association consumer website has a section on Special Needs cruising.

• Type www.discover-cruising.co.uk into the Address bar.

• Press **Enter**.

• Scroll down to the Cruises For You section.

• Click on **Special Needs Cruises**.

• Click on **Print Fact Sheet**.

More useful links:

• **www.accessibletravel.co.uk** Packages and cruises worldwide. They can even arrange specialist shore excursions.

• **www.cruisingholiday.co.uk** Featuring over 2,000 disabled-friendly cruises.

There are also discussion boards on cruising for the disabled at CruiseCritic.com.

- Type www.cruisecritic.com into the Address bar.

- Press **Enter**.

- Click on the **Boards** link on the bar across the top of the home page.

- Scroll down to the section on Special Interest Cruising.

- Click on **Disabled Cruise Travel**.

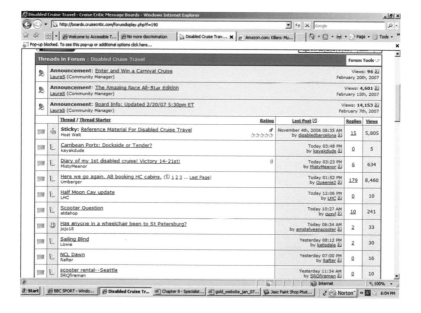

More information

The government's own website has some valuable pages.

- Type **www.direct.gov.uk** into the Address bar.
- Press **Enter**.

- Click on the **Disabled people** link under the People section.
- Scroll down to the Travel, holidays and breaks section.
- Click on **Holidays in the UK for disabled people**.

Pay special attention

Make sure your insurance policy or travel insurance covers pre-existing conditions. Be aware that travel insurance often excludes wheelchair and equipment coverage.

More general links:

- **www.access-able.com** American site dedicated to aiding travellers with disabilities.

- **www.flying-with-disability.org** Advice regarding flights.

- **www.medicaltravel.org** American company specialising in mobility product rentals.

- **www.radar.co.uk** Royal Association for Disability and Rehabilitation.

Solo travellers

Typically, solo holidaymakers have had a bad deal from mainstream holiday companies. Single supplements (where many packages are based on two people sharing a hotel room) and limited availability have made it hard to find a good package at a sensible price.

But there are now companies specialising in the single traveller, and this is of particular note to the over-50s, many of whom are put off by exorbitant supplements and other complications.

The directory

By far the most useful site in this area is Singular Travel, which has partnered with dozens of regular tour operators to provide good rates for single travellers, especially the older generation.

- However, it is a site you need to register for, so start by going to **www.singulartravel.co.uk**.

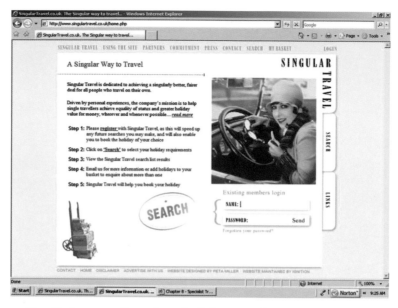

- Scroll down to Step 1 and click on **register**.

- Enter the essential details (marked with an asterisk).

- Choose a user name and password.

- Non-asterisked details are all optional.
- Enter your Travel Preferences, which is where the site can really help you.

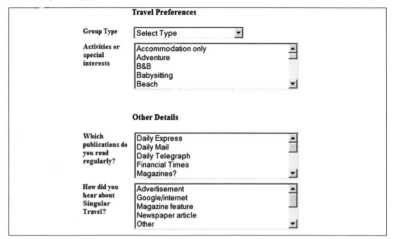

- Under Group Type, you can select from 12 categories, from No Preference to Over 50s.
- You can then choose from a longer list of Activities or special interests.
- To select multiple activities that interest you, press **Ctrl** and left-click the mouse (Mac users press the 'apple' key and click).
- The Other Details are optional.
- Click in the 'I agree to Terms & Conditions' box.
- Click on **Save** at the bottom of the page.
- You can then go on to search the site.

- Click on the **Search** section among the links down the left side of every page.

- You are given a selection of dozens of Activities which you can match up with desired Countries (or just leave the Country section blank for the widest selection).

- You can select a Season or enter your Departure and Return dates separately, and stipulate the price range you are looking for.

- Click the **Search** button and you will usually get several pages of results.

- Select **Click here for more details** to see the full details.

- You can then use their **E-mail Singular Travel** link at the foot of the page to ask for any more details you may require.

More information

- **www.adventurecompany.co.uk** Adventure travel with no single supplement fees. Automatic room sharing with same-sex group member.

- **www.justyou.co.uk** Singles focused; age range 30–70.

- **www.saga.co.uk/travel** Specialise in over 50s, with a brochure for singles only, but singles travel cannot be booked online; go to the Request a brochure section and order the Holidays for Single Travellers brochure or call 0800 414 444.

- **www.solosholidays.co.uk** Group-led UK short breaks and worldwide travel for age ranges 25–45, 30–59 and 45+.

- **www.travel-quest.co.uk** Singles holidays or women-only sections.

Your reminder box

- Be specific in your search terms for adventure holidays.

- Use the directory **www.travel-quest.co.uk** for a wide range of possibilities.

- Be prepared to ask questions of smaller travel companies.

- Do *a lot* of research before embarking on something like a gap year.

- Use practical advice sites like **www.inmyprime.co.uk** and **www.access-able.com**.

- For single travellers, use the specialist sites rather than the mainstream companies for the best deals.

Chapter 8

Buying Safely

Providing your credit card details and committing to a purchase can be the most intimidating issue when booking travel online. Millions of people do it every day and it isn't hard to make safe purchases if you know what to look for.

We will point you in the right direction so you feel secure in knowing you have booked with a reputable company in the first place, and know what to do if you run into problems.

Knowing who to trust

Those logos you see at the bottom of a web page are important keys to knowing who is insuring that your transaction is protected.

ABTA: Association of British Travel Agents. A UK bonding company who guarantee the security of your money when booking a holiday with a travel agent or tour operator who has ABTA membership.

- Look for the ABTA logo at the bottom of the main page when booking a package holiday.

- Click on **the logo** to be sure it links to ABTA's website, which is further confirmation of their affiliation with the site you are using.

AITO: Association of Independent Tour Operators. A bonding and security agency representing some of Britain's specialist tour operators.

ATOL: Air Travel Organisers Licensing. A UK bonding company who guarantee the security of your money when booking a flight. All tour operators who include flights as part of their package must have an ATOL licence to operate.

- Look for the ATOL logo at the bottom of the main page when booking flights.

IATA: International Air Transport Association. They do not work directly with consumer security but are a trade association representing the airline industry. You may not see their logo, but they represent 94 per cent of international scheduled air travel carriers.

Making safe payments

Worrying as it may seem, a few simple observations will soon tell you if your payment is being handled safely.

- Look for a closed padlock icon (or unbroken key) in the bottom right corner of your browser or next to the Address bar.

- Click on the padlock icon for confirmation it is active.

- A closed padlock on the website itself is meaningless. It must appear in your browser.

- Look for a change from 'http' to 'https' in the web address in your Address bar to ensure the website has become secure and your details are being encrypted.

Don't worry **about credit card information**

As long as you are using a secure site, it is safe to give your credit card information when making purchases. If you feel particularly nervous about the whole idea, reputable companies will offer to take your order by phone. Look for that option as you make your way through the booking process.

More ways to shop safely

- Use well-known booking agents such as Expedia, Travelocity or ebookers.

- Book directly through a specific airline, tour operator, car hire or accommodation website.

- Make note of an alternate means of contacting the company in case of a problem or dispute. Reputable online companies will display a postal address and phone number, usually under Contact Us.

- Friends, relatives and online forums are a good resource for asking questions about a company's quality, price and customer service.

- As they say, if an offer looks too good to be true, it probably is. While the occasional bargain can be found for hundreds of pounds less at one site than at others, the chances are there are strings attached. Always read the fine print to be sure you know exactly what you're getting. Some deals are a straightforward saving; most are something other than they appear at first glance.

Contact Us

Contact Customer Service by e-mail.

Please use the e-mail address associated with your Amazon.co.uk account.

[By e-mail]

Talk to Customer Service by phone.

Provide your phone number and we'll call you right away.

[Note: this feature is currently available for customers in the UK and Ireland only.]

[By phone]

- Print out the payment confirmation page, which will have a transaction/ reference number in case of problems.

- Print out the Terms and Conditions page if you wish.

Don't worry **about PayPal and WorldPay**

Some websites will process your payment through an 'e-commerce service' such as PayPal or WorldPay. They are both well-established companies which act as the middleman between the buyer and the seller as regards payment, but do not otherwise affect your purchase.

- Check your credit card statement as soon as you receive it. If you find a transaction you did not make or an incorrect payment amount, contact your credit card company immediately and place the payment in dispute until you are able to sort it out with the online company.

Pay special attention

No reputable company will ever ask for the PIN number or password to your bank account. Never, under any circumstances, give anyone that information. Your credit card details are all that is needed for online transactions.

Cooling-off period

In all the excitement of planning, you may book something only to have second thoughts about it later. Your consumer's rights guarantee you a 'cooling off period' after making a purchase (usually seven working days), during which time you can ask for a refund without giving a reason. Beware: some businesses (notably, airlines) are exempt from this regulation. Always check the terms and conditions for specifics. Check the Department of Trade and Industry for more on your consumer rights.

- Type www.dti.gov.uk into the Address bar.

- Click the **Confident Consumers** link.

ABOUT DTI	▶ **Better Business Framework**	▶ **Europe & World Trade**
CONTACT	▶ **Business Sectors**	▶ **Innovation**
HELP WITH THIS SITE	▶ **Employment Matters**	▶ **Regional Economic Development**
SITE INDEX	▶ **Energy**	▶ **Science**
23rd February 2007	▶ **Confident Consumers** - A Fair Deal creating Prosperity & Success for All	

- Click on **Fact Sheets** in the menu along the left side.

Business Activities
Buying & Selling
Consumers, Estate
Agents and Redress
Bill
Consumer Finance
Consumer Law
Enforcement
Consumer Policy
Consumer Safety
Consumer Support
Fact Sheets

- Click on the **Distance Selling** link in the alphabetical directory.

Also visit:

- Consumer Direct at **www.consumerdirect.gov.uk**.

Your reminder box

- ABTA and ATOL are good logos to look for as added security.

- Look for a closed padlock or unbroken key in your browser or next to the Address bar.

- The web address will change from http to https when the site becomes secure.

- WorldPay and PayPal act as a middleman between the buyer and the seller when it comes to payment. Your transaction will not otherwise be affected.

- Print out your payment confirmation page.

- Always read the Terms and Conditions before buying.

- You may have a cooling-off period with some purchases.

- When you feel comfortable with the information you have, book your holiday with confidence.

Chapter 9

Destinations

You are ready to seek out websites which give specific information about the location you will be visiting and this is where using the internet really gets exciting. Don't be afraid to have fun with it!

In Chapter 2 we learned about the resources for researching your destination. Now we can use them. The skills you gained using search engines and directories will come in handy as you look for destination-specific websites. This section will help you to become comfortable with the research process as we work through some examples.

Tourist offices

Official tourist office websites are a good place to start. They generally include basic information to help narrow your focus regarding accommodation, attractions, events, dining, shopping and transportation in the location you choose.

Don't worry about no tourism office

The USA does not have an official tourism office. Each state is responsible for its own tourism. Use the state name (such as, "Tourist Office" New York) when entering your search terms.

In this example we will use GoogleUK to find a Tourist Office for travel within the United Kingdom.

- Type www.google.co.uk into the Address bar.

- Type "UK Tourist Office" in the Google Search box and press **Enter**.

- The first result is Your official guide to Britain – Visit Britain.

- Click on the link.

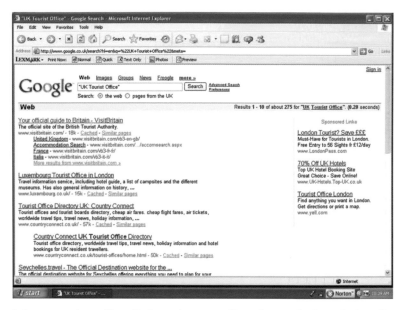

Most tourist office links take you directly to their website. In this case, you may first be taken to a directory where you must choose a region. If so,

• Scroll down until you see the United Kingdom link.

• Click on the link.

• The VisitBritain main page will appear.

From VisitBritain's main page, narrow your search by clicking on the appropriate link to your destination or by using the Destination Guides tab at the top of the page.

Many tourist office websites are more straightforward, with obvious links to the main features of their locations. Sites that cover a specific city or area rather than an entire country tend to be more user-friendly.

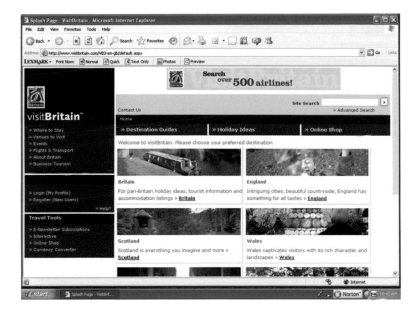

Cumbria Tourist Board's website is a good example.

* Type "Tourist Office" Cumbria into a GoogleUK Search box, leaving Cumbria outside quotation marks.

* The first link is for the Cumbria Tourism Board's official website.

* Click on the **Cumbria and Lake District Tourist Board for Holidays in Cumbria** link.

* The main page for Cumbria and the Lake District will appear.

Don't worry **about pushing buttons**

It's time to have fun with your research! Click on each link that appeals to you when searching a website. Check other destinations within your general location and don't be afraid to explore. You can always return to the main page by clicking on the black arrow to the right of your Back button. Links to the last pages you viewed will drop down in the menu box. Look for the main page link and click on it.

- Begin exploring by clicking on **See & Do** (or similar terminology, depending on the website), which has links to attractions, events, shopping, dining and more.

Useful links:

- **www.europe.org** Official tourist office for Europe with links to specific countries' official tourist offices.

- **www.infoplease.com** USA State and Territory tourism office directory.

- **www.towd.com** Tourism Offices Worldwide Directory.

Official travel advice

Whether you are travelling within the UK or abroad it is important to have up-to-date public service information regarding security, health matters, transportation regulations and local laws and customs.

UK government travel advice

The Foreign & Commonwealth Office issues official travel advice, along with current warnings listed by country.

- Type www.fco.gov.uk into the Address bar.

- The Foreign & Commonwealth Office main page appears.

- Click on **Travel Advice** on the left side of the screen, under Services.

- The Travel Advice page appears with links down the left-hand side of the screen.

- Click on each topic of interest for the latest updates and advice covering nearly all aspects of travel.

Directgov, produced by the Central Office of Information, is another useful website. We will use it as an example of how to find a travel office using a search engine.

- Type www.google.co.uk in the Address bar.

- Type "official travel advice" in the Google Search box.

- The link entitled Travelling Abroad: Directgov – Travel and Transport is a UK government produced site (note the designation *gov.uk* in the link's address).

- Click on the link or open in a new browser window.

- Directgov's Travelling abroad page appears, with links grouped by category.

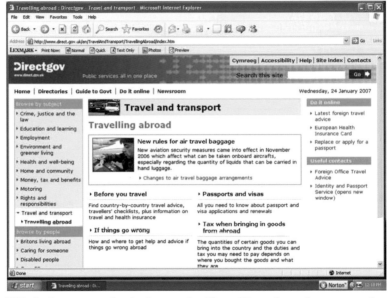

While browsing the links on the Travelling abroad page, notice the panel down the left-hand side of the screen which allows you to Browse by people.

- Click on the **Over 50s** link.

- Click on the **Travel and leisure** link for travel advice geared towards seniors.

> **There's more!**
>
> Directgov offers a wealth of lifestyle information in a section devoted to seniors. Visit **www.directgov.uk** and click on the **Over 50s** link on the home page.

Guidebooks

An informative guidebook is like taking a trusted friend along when you travel. While the majority of your research can be done online, there is nothing like having a good guidebook to read during your journey and while you tour.

Many popular guidebook series can be found at your local bookshop or on the internet, where Amazon has all the best titles with the convenience of safe, one-stop shopping.

• Type www.amazon.co.uk in the Address bar.

• Open the drop-down menu next to the Search button by clicking on the arrow next to it.

• Click on **Books**.

• If you know the title you are looking for, type it into the Search box. If not, type in Travel Guides.

• Press **Enter**.

• The list generated will be in order of greatest sales, with the best selling titles at the top.

- Narrow your search by typing specific terms in the search box, such as Travel Guides Australia or City Guides New York. Amazon is forgiving. You do not need quote marks around your search terms to generate successful results.

Some of the more popular guidebook series are:

- **Brit's Guides:** We're partial to these since we write two titles, which are usually the best-sellers for their destinations: *A Brit's Guide to Orlando* and *A Brit's Guide to Disneyland Paris*. Simon also writes *A Brit's Guide to Choosing A Cruise*. Other titles include *Top 50 Ski and Snowboard Resorts in Europe*, *A Brit's Guide to New York* and *A Brit's Guide to Las Vegas*.

- **Dorling Kindersley (DK):** 93 well-illustrated travel guides in the Eyewitness Series, 41 in the Top Ten series and 8 city guides in the Real City series.

- **Fodors:** Five travel-related series including the Fodor's Gold Guides, the See It Guides and Citypack Guides.

- **Frommer's:** 16 travel-related series such as Day By Day, Dirt

Cheap and Free, National Parks and the Frommer's Portable titles, with several locations in each series.

- **Lonely Planet:** Six destination series under Best of Guides, Shoestring Guides, City, Country and Regional Guides and Citiescapes titles.
- **Time Out:** 90 titles under the Time Out brand.

While shopping for travel guides, don't forget to pick up a phrase book!

There's more!

Once you create an account, Amazon will remember your preferences and provide a list of recommendations based on the items you have viewed or purchased. It will appear beside your name at the top of the page.

Another useful link:

- **www.stanfords.co.uk** Specialist travel bookshop.

Travel review websites

Travel review websites are another key element in the 'social internet' research toolbox, meaning they rely on members to share experiences and post opinions. While some sites (such as Trip Advisor) closely monitor reviews for accuracy, most accept members' views without question.

Opinions regarding all things holiday-related are a valuable resource in planning and are especially helpful when there are several reviews on the same topic, ideally on more than one site.

Finding travel review sites

Search for review sites based on specific criteria (car hire or hotels) or general criteria such as destination. The steps are essentially the same, only the search terms change. Some examples are:

- For a specific topic, try search terms like "hire car" reviews.

- For accommodation in a specific location try terms such as "hotel reviews" Las Vegas.

- For general destination reviews try terms like "Travel Reviews" Switzerland.

Pay special attention

If a review seems too positive or reads like a holiday brochure, it was possibly posted by someone who works at the destination in question. Conversely, one bad review among many good ones could indicate someone with a personal axe to grind.

Enter almost any search term for travel reviews and the top website will be Trip Advisor. It is widely considered to be the best, and we like the fact reviews are monitored for accuracy. There are many others worth checking and we think it is important to find two or three you like for a wider variety of opinions.

Trip Advisor

Covering more than 30,000 destinations worldwide and with more than 20 million members, Trip Advisor is the largest online review site and well worth adding to your Favorites list.

- Type www.tripadvisor.co.uk into the Address bar.

- Search by destination using the map on the right of the screen.

Browse Destinations

United States | Mexico | Caribbean | Europe
Canada | Africa | Asia | Middle East
Central America | South America | South Pacific

- Or click on **Read and Write Reviews**.
- Enter your destination in the Search box and press **Enter**.

There's more!

Trip Advisor also has a section called goLists, where travellers post tips on destinations they know well. They are often worth reading. Look for the goLists link on the main page.

Holiday Watchdog

A useful site with a British perspective. Smaller than Trip Advisor, some locations listed on Holiday Watchdog may not have reviews yet. But it is easy to navigate and the content is generally accurate. This site is not connected with the BBC's *Watchdog* TV programme.

- Type www.holidaywatchdog.com in the Address bar.
- Search using destination tabs at the top of the page.
- Or enter a destination using the Search box and press **Enter**.

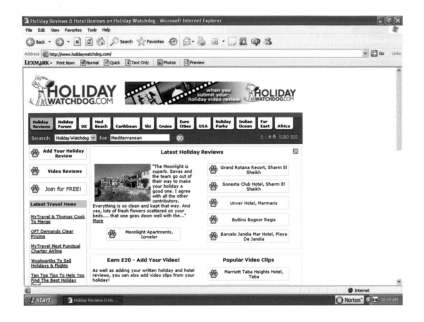

There's more!

Click on the **Video Reviews** link on the left-hand side of the main page for high-quality streaming video clips of select accommodation from around the world. Enormously useful for viewing the grounds, pool and accommodation interior, which can be reassuring before you book.

Virtual Tourist

Virtual Tourist takes the review concept one step further. After reading each review, members may post questions or comments, add tips and rate the review, making it easier to search by a star system for those that are most useful. The site is loaded with destination information, including forums and a Trip Planner.

• Type www.virtualtourist.com into the Address bar.

• Click on your desired region using the map on the main page.

- Click on your desired country using the map on the next page, or click on your desired country or city using the list on the right.

- Scroll down past the Sponsored Links to find reviews.

- Click on the review you wish to read.

More travel review sites:

- **www.iExplore.com** Reviews, journals and pictures. Search by region, country and activity.

- **www.lonelyplanet.com/bluelist** Travel recommendations, tips and secrets.

- **www.myholidayreport.com** Text-only reviews, some areas covered better than others.

- **www.realtravel.com** Hotel, dining and sights reviews.

- **www.worldtravelguide.net** International city guides.

Travel forums

Discussion forums (or discussion boards), can be one of the most useful destination research tools on the web, offering up-to-the-minute information, a wealth of first-hand reviews and the priceless benefit of being able to ask questions of real people and (usually) receive helpful answers.

Because there are few restrictions regarding who can post (internet-speak for 'ask or reply to questions') on a forum, information can sometimes be sketchy or downright incorrect. Usually, other members will correct inaccuracies but there is nothing like doing your own research, using forum information as a starting point.

Good words to know

Moderator: A person, usually a volunteer, responsible for making sure discussion forum rules are followed and threads stay on-topic and respectful.

Post: The act of creating and submitting a new topic or replying to a topic ('I'm going to post a question about Paris, France'). Also, the topic itself ('I read an informative post about river cruises').

Smilies: Those cute little icons that help get your intended emotion across. Sometimes called emoticons.

Subject line: The title of a thread ('The subject line indicates the thread is about camping in Wyoming').

Thread: A new post and all of its subsequent replies ('There is a thread on the Africa forum with 16 replies').

How to find a good internet forum

Finding a travel forum can be as easy as typing "Travel forums" into a Search box and perusing the resulting list. If you're looking for discussions on a specific kind of holiday ("Camping forums") or a location ("Travel forums" New

Zealand), enter search terms geared towards those requirements. You are bound to find some gems, but you are also likely to run across forums whose information borders on useless.

Rather than spending weeks reading forums, here are a few steps to show how accurate replies might be and, therefore, how useful the forum.

* Think of a destination you know well (for us, it's Orlando, Florida).

* When you visit a forum for the first time, begin by looking at several posts concerning that destination.

* If the replies are accurate, you may want to read further or sign up as a member.

* If the replies are largely inaccurate (or, even worse, rude, flippant or disrespectful) move to another forum.

* Check the dates on the latest posts. The more recent the posts on the first page of a discussion board, the more active that forum is. If there are posts dating back weeks or months on the first page, move on to a busier forum or risk frustration waiting for an answer to your questions.

Don't worry about being the 'newbie'

Many web forums have a Help section or a Frequently Asked Questions page for 'newbies' (new members). Once you have registered as a member, everything you need to know about posting, etiquette and each forum's rules can be found on the FAQ page.

Well-known travel forums

While well-known forums may or may not be the best option for your specific location, they are tried and tested when it comes to giving good advice, making them an excellent starting point – or even the only forums you visit. You can even ask fellow members to suggest other forums specific to your location. One of the best Disney websites we know of came on the recommendation of a member at another, better-known forum. Sometimes smaller forums are the friendliest and most useful.

Fodor's forums

- Type www.fodors.com/forums into the Address bar.
- Look at the Select A Forum list down the left-hand side of the screen.

- Click on the location you wish to research.
- A list of existing topics will appear down the left of the screen.

- Browse this list for questions or topics similar to your own.

- Alternatively, browse topics within your location by typing keywords (such as safaris or restaurants) into the Search box at the top of the page.

- Select a location from the drop-down menu and click **Search**.

- Click on the topic you would like to read.

- Remember, you must register as a member to post your own questions and reply to other questions.

Lonely Planet

- Type www.lonelyplanet.com into the Address bar.

- Click on **Thorn Tree Forum** in the column down the left of the screen.

- You will have a choice of 51 forums, including specialised topics (Older Travellers, Women Travellers, On Your Bike, Diving & Snorkelling and much more), community orientated forums (sports, culture, food) and even a forum dedicated to the ethics of travel. The screenshot below is a small sample.

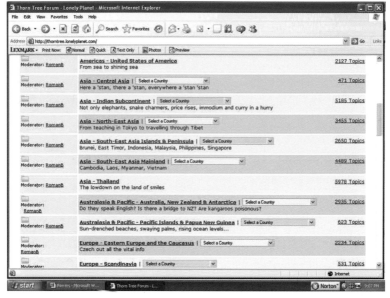

- Click on the links to any forums that appeal to you.

- The most recently posted threads (topics) for that location or category will appear, one below the other, with a replies link in the lower right corner of each topic.

- Click on the **replies** link to see more posts responding to the original post.

Don't worry about off-colour topics

Almost every forum will have the occasional off-colour joke or rough language. Many forums have moderators who remove objectionable posts, but some are more relaxed about profanity than others. The best thing to do if a post offends is use your Back button and stop reading. If you come across several inappropriate topics on a forum it may be best to find another website.

More travel forums:

- **www.aardvarktravel.net/chat/** 31 forums, covering 14 regions, 9 categories (including one for Space Travel!) and 4 community topics (food, health, equipment, companions).

- **www.travellerspoint.com/forum.cfm** Small, but friendly and knowledgeable.

- **www.tripadvisor.co.uk/ForumHome** Includes Airline, Cruise, Adventure Travel forums and more.

- **www.virtualtourist.com** A large selection of forums, some areas covered better than others.

Practical use of travel forums

Internet forums are like clubs. They each have their own 'personality' and the best forums give members a real sense of belonging to a unique community. When you find one you like and decide to become a member, there are a few basic steps to get started.

Registering as a member

- Click on the registration button or link. It may be labelled Register, Join, New Members or similar.

- Follow instructions for registering, selecting a user name and password. We suggest choosing a user name that is not your real name (such as Travelbug or CharltonFan) or a shortened version of your name (IanW). Do not use your full name.

- You will be required to provide an e-mail address.

Pay special attention

You may want to set up a free e-mail account with **hotmail.co.uk** or **yahoo.co.uk** just for things such as forum registrations, but it is generally safe to give your primary e-mail address when registering. Check the forum's privacy terms if you are unsure.

- You may need to confirm your registration. Some websites will send an e-mail to the account you have specified, providing a link you must click on to activate your account.

- Then, begin posting!

Don't worry **about all those letters**

One of the first things you notice when reading discussion boards is language which seems to be in code. When confronted with statements such as 'My BIL, AKA Larry, had me LOL at his DD's reaction to FOTLK', you may be tempted to hit the Back button. But wait! The forum usually has an Abbreviations page, which will help you decode all those letters. Another option is to ignore abbreviations you don't understand. Often they are irrelevant chatter.

What does our example sentence say? It reads: 'My brother in law, also known as Larry, had me laughing out loud at his dear daughter's reaction to Festival of the Lion King (stage show)'.

Posting questions on an internet forum

- Click on the **Sign In** (Log In) link on the forum's main page.

- Enter your user name and password.

- Click on the link to the specific forum you wish to post your message in.

- Look for **Post New Topic** or **New Thread** and click on it.

- Type a meaningful title in the Subject box that represents your specific question (such as: Need Oslo hotel recommendations rather than Need Help).
- Type your question in the Text box provided. Be as specific as possible, including the month or season you are travelling, which area you will visit and so on.

- Click **Submit** (or Post Message, etc).

Don't worry **about getting fancy**

Those little smiley faces many people use on forums are cute, but you're here for information. When you are more comfortable with basic navigation, you can experiment with adding coloured text, smilies, quotes and more – if that appeals to you.

Forum etiquette

Every forum has its own rules. Most are common sense, but some are less obvious.

- Be sure to read the Rules for Posting.

- Do not type in capital letters. IT LOOKS LIKE YOU ARE SHOUTING!

- Never give personal information (phone number, address, password etc.).

- If a thread annoys you, hit the Back button.

- In a nutshell, be nice.

Webcams

Webcams may have limited value as research tools but they are great fun for increasing pre-holiday excitement and nearly as much fun afterwards for those wistful 'wish we were there' moments.

Good words to know

Streaming video: Video that moves in 'real time' rather than still shots that update periodically.

Thumbnail: Small pictures which, when clicked on, become big pictures. In the case of webcam sites, thumbnails often link to that webcam location and corresponding web pages.

Travel-Webcams

A fabulous resource with nearly 2,200 webcams all over the world, including six cruise ships.

- Type www.travel-webcams.com into the Address bar.
- Click on your location from the list on the main page.

- A list of available webcams comes up, with thumbnails of each location.
- Click on the thumbnail picture to view the webcam.
- You will be redirected to a website corresponding to the webcam location you have chosen.
- To return to the thumbnail list, click your **Back** button.
- To return to Travel-Webcams, click on the black arrow next to your Back button, then click on the **Travel-Webcams The Outdoor-Webcam-Directory** link.

BBC

The BBC website **www.bbc.co.uk/webcams** has hundreds of webcams from around England, Scotland and Wales.

- Click on the drop-down menu arrow next to the box that has the words A–Z of BBC Webcams in it, for a list of webcams.

- Click on the location you want to view.

- You may have to click **Go** or you may be automatically forwarded to the page you have requested.

- A pop-up box will appear with a still shot taken from the webcam you have chosen.

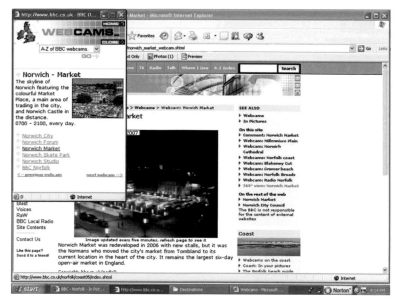

- There may or may not be further webcam selections for the location you have chosen, listed in the pop-up box.

- The main Webcam page will also change, redirecting you to a web page corresponding to the webcam you have chosen.

> **There's more!**
>
> The web page you have been redirected to may also have several additional links to webcams specific to the area you have chosen to view.

- To close the pop-up box, click on the red X in the upper right corner of the screen.

- To return to the main Webcam page, click on the **Back** button at the upper left-hand corner of the redirected page.

- If you have visited other pages on the redirected website and want to return to the main page, click on the black arrow next to your Back button, then click on the link that reads **BBC-Webcams**.

Don't worry **about red Xs and black screens**

Some webcams display a box with a red X in the upper left corner of the screen, where the picture should be. This indicates the camera is currently not working and isn't usually a problem with your computer. When you see a black screen where the picture should be, remember it may well be night time in the location you have chosen. This is common with beach and cruise ship cams that have been directed towards the sea.

Kroooz-Cams

This site offers 73 BridgeCams from 12 cruise lines and 76 PortCams. Navigation is easy.

- Type www.kroooz-cams.com (note spelling) into the Address bar.

- Click on the cruise line or port you are interested in.

- Select the area you'd like to view from the drop-down list.

- Some locations have additional webcam links under the webcam you have selected. In the screenshot below, you can see links to Bora Bora, Moorea, Manihi and Tahaa directly under the webcam screen.

There's more!

Kroooz-Cams.Com even has a handy Multi-Cam Viewer, which allows you to view two BridgeCams, two PortCams and a Fullsize Cam at the same time. Select the five webcams you would like to see by using the drop-down menu under each webcam screen.

Google Earth

This is more like the ultimate webcam. Zoom in on anywhere on the planet for an up-close view. It feels like you are flying and is highly addictive. You have to download the Google Earth program, but it's safe and free.

* Type www.googleearth.com into your Address bar.

* Look for the green Download button. Click on it once.

* Follow the instructions that appear in the pop-up box.

* Click on **Run** rather than Save, when prompted.

* Navigate by scrolling around using your mouse.

* If you have a little wheel between the left and right button on your mouse this will zoom you in or out. Try it! (Not available on Mac systems.)

* Or enter a location or address into the Search box.

More webcam links:

- **www.camvista.com** Worldwide webcams by location or category (such as pubs or animals).

- **www.snoweye.com** Worldwide ski resort webcams.

- **www.webcamgalore.com** More than 2,300 webcams worldwide.

Travel blogs

A shortened version of 'web log', blog refers to mini-travelogues written by travellers recording their experiences through text and photos. Writing skills vary, but the best blogs are filled with the sort of information and excitement that makes readers want to join the adventure.

Good word to know

Blogger: A person who writes a web log. Many travel bloggers post their personal journal (blog) when taking extended journeys.

Finding travel blogs

- Type www.google.co.uk into the Address bar.
- For general blogs, type in "Travel Blogs".
- For blogs on a specific region, try terms like "travel blogs" Europe.
- Scroll through the results, clicking on any links that appeal to you.

There's more!

Type Blogs into a Google Search box. The first result will be Google Blog Search. Click on the link, then type Travel into the Blog Search box. Google will return a list of recently posted blogs within your search category.

Travelblog

Travelblog offers the perfect blend of rich text, captivating photos and thoughtful, informative blogs that whisk readers away with the feeling that you are really there.

- Type www.travelblog.org in the Address bar.

- Search by region clicking on the labelled tabs or map on the main page.

- On the next page, click on the map or the link to the area you want.

- Click on the link to your chosen area's blogs, at the upper left of the page. For example, if you chose Europe and France, the link will read France Travel Blogs.

- Some locations allow you to narrow your search further, with links to cities or territories.

More travel blogs:

- **www.blogtopsites.com/travel** Blog directory.

- **www.IgoUgo.com** Huge database of blogs from around the world.

- **www.realtravel.com** Click on the **Travel Blogs** link at the bottom of the main page.

- **www.travellerspoint.com** From the main page click on the **Blogs** link.

Podcasts

Think of podcasts as a free radio broadcast over your computer's speakers. You choose the topic, when to listen and can even pause the show to freshen up your tea.

As a research tool, podcasts offer insider knowledge about a location, such as the top ten sites in Venice, how to order food in Italian and what is available in the local street market. Just as blogs are a text and photo travelogue, podcasts are audio tours that can be just as compelling.

Finding travel podcasts

As with all searches, you can use Google, Yahoo or your favourite search engine, entering terms such as:

* Travel podcasts
* "podcasts" Egypt (or Las Vegas, backpackers, etc.)
* "podcast directories" Travel

Don't worry about ActiveX pop-ups

You may get a pop-up box that says 'Click to run an ActiveX control on this webpage' when you select the podcast you want to hear. Click on it; if you already have ActiveX on your computer, nothing new will be downloaded. If not, you may be prompted to download it. ActiveX is safe and can be downloaded with confidence. Visit **www.activex.com** for the free download if you don't have it.

Podcast.net

An example of a podcast directory, this can be used to search for audio tours for specific locations or travel-related topics.

* Type www.podcast.net into the Address bar.
* Select **Keywords** from the drop-down box next to the Search box on the main page.
* Type your desired location into the Search box (such as Morocco or Edinburgh).

- Browse the descriptions under each result for travel-related podcasts.

Alternatively, type Travel in the Search box on the main page and browse all travel-related topics. You can also access the Travel section by clicking on the link labelled **Travel** under the heading Hobbies and Recreation on the main page.

Pay special attention

Many research websites you are likely to use will have podcasts, blogs and forums. Be sure to look for tabs or links to these 'extras' as you browse review sites, official information sites and other travel-related sites.

More podcasts:

- **www.lonelyplanet.com/podcasts** Wonderfully descriptive stories. Limited selection.

- **www.podcastdirectory.com/format/Travel** Directory of travel-related podcasts.

Your reminder box

- Official tourist offices are a good starting point for basic location information.

- Public service information, such as travel and health warnings, laws and transportation information can be found at official travel advice sites.

- Guidebooks make handy take-along reference guides and often provide insider information about the location you are visiting.

- Review sites are helpful in the decision-making stage, offering advice from real people on hotels, dining and more.

- Beware of overly positive or negative replies on review sites.

- Travel forums are a great resource for asking specific questions.

- Don't believe everything you read on forums. Use replies to your question as a starting point, then do your own research.

- You must register to post on a forum or review site. It is generally safe and free.

- Webcams allow you to see part of the area or resort you will be visiting before you go.

- Blogs often contain a great deal of insight into a specific location as bloggers tend to record trips in detail.

- Podcasts serve as audio tours, which may contain useful insider tips.

- Never give out personal information (address, phone number, etc.) on a discussion forum and keep your password confidential.

Chapter 10
Package Holidays

There may be occasions when you do not have the time or the inclination to research and book each element of your holiday separately. Perhaps you just feel more comfortable letting someone else do the work in arranging the details. It is a perfectly valid (and popular) option to keep things simple by choosing a package over the DIY option.

What to look for

Even if you are booking a straightforward package, there will be some additional elements and booking considerations to bear in mind as you work through the various searches.

But, at its most basic, to find a package holiday:

- Type "Package holidays" into a GoogleUK Search box (remembering to click on the **Pages from the UK** option). If you already know where you want to go, include your destination (e.g. "Package holidays" Tenerife).

Good words to know

Fly-drive: A package combination of flight and car hire for a destination (very common in Florida and the USA) but not including accommodation.

Multi-centre (or twin centre): A combination package holiday to more than one location, either within the same country or in nearby countries. Typical examples are an Orlando and beach resort combination in Florida, and a safari and beach resort holiday in Africa.

Touring holiday: A conducted group tour (usually by coach) around various regions e.g. New England in the autumn or the Battlefields of World War I.

- Alternatively, go straight to one of the big online travel agents (Expedia, LastMinute or Travelcare) and click on their Holidays tab, as opposed to Flights, Accommodation, Attractions or Car Hire (NB: with Expedia.co.uk, after clicking on Holidays, you then need to select the Brochure Packages option).

- If you know which tour operator you want to travel with, seek out their specific website (e.g. **www.airtours.co.uk** or **www.virginholidays.co.uk**).

- You can also search by other holiday choices – Winter Sun, Beach Holidays, Skiing, All-Inclusive, Fly-Drives, Worldwide (for more exotic destinations), Mediterranean, Florida, etc.

Finding the best price

There are several key elements to bear in mind when booking a package:

* Book as early as possible. Many operators have discounts for the earliest bookers, especially if you want a specific destination.

* Book as late as possible. OK, that may sound a complete contradiction but, if you are happy to take a more limited selection and go at relatively short notice, you can pick up a bargain. Operators will often cut prices on some packages from 1–10 weeks before the departure date if they are just not selling well.

* Pick off-peak times. This is especially important for package holidays, which are heavily weighted towards the main holiday periods.

For the big mass-market holidays, destinations like the Spanish Costas, the Canaries and even Florida (at times) still tend to be cheaper as a tour operator package than a DIY option.

The other benefit of a package over DIY is that you are booking through a specific tour operator who should have full ATOL protection (see Chapter 8). That means, if the holiday company were to go bust, you will either get a refund or, if you are already away, you will be able to complete your holiday.

If you have booked all your elements separately and one of them fails, it is unlikely you will get a refund on everything.

Getting advance notice of the deals

Many travel agent websites have an e-mail option that enables them to notify you as soon as special deals and bargain offers become available, and they are worth signing up for.

* For example, on Expedia.co.uk, go to their Holidays section and, in the small menu on the left under the heading Traveller Tools, click the link that says **Get deals by e-mail**.

- Enter your e-mail address in the 'Sign up here' box and click **Submit**. Then be ready for a barrage of e-mails to roll in offering deals to everywhere!

Most agents offer this feature, and it is worth signing up with a couple if you *really* want to study those advance offers.

Package price 'extras'

It used to be the case that a package holiday really was a complete package and the bottom line figure was what you paid. Sadly, that isn't always the case these days and you need to be aware of a few not quite so optional extras.

- The biggest thing to watch out for is whether transfers from your destination airport to your accommodation are included. It is not uncommon for operators to charge extra for transfers, so find this out during the booking process.

- Tour operators with charter airlines will also charge for in-flight extras. These can include pre-bookable seats (to ensure you can sit together), extra-legroom seats and even in-flight meals. Obviously you can decline to pay for their little plastic meal and take your own snacks for the flight, but you need to be aware of these options at the booking stage.

• Travel insurance will usually be a booking option, and you may even need to uncheck the box to ensure it is not included in your quote (it is nearly always cheaper to buy your travel insurance elsewhere – see Chapter 14).

Searching by tour operator

If you are happy to stick with one particular tour operator, either from personal experience or from friend or family recommendations, the simplest thing is just to go to that operator's website.

Typically, you can either choose from some of the highlighted options, or input your own details and click **Search**.

Say you are looking to go to Tenerife for a week and prefer to use Airtours holidays.

• Type www.airtours.co.uk into the Address bar.

• Under Airtours' list of Sun Deals, click on the **Tenerife** link.

- Sometimes the link will take you directly to a selection of package choices, more often it will take you to another menu where you need to input your date requirements.

- If your dates are flexible, several pages of choices are likely to come up, especially with popular destinations.

Pay special attention

Always double-check that the departure airport for the package is still the same as the one you require. Sometimes search engines can default to different search criteria for reasons of their own!

If the results are too overwhelming, narrow your search.

- Click on the **Back** button.

- Refine your search terms under the Hotel rating and Board basis (e.g. AAAA for the former and Half-board for the latter).

- When you are happy with your choice, click on **Get quote**.

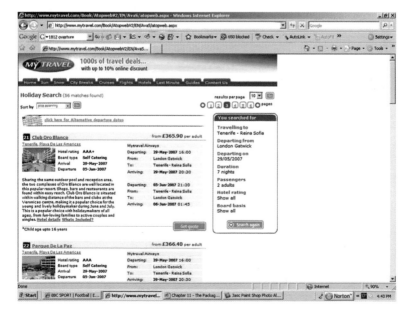

- It is not uncommon for the figure displayed to change once you get the full quote. In this instance the price actually goes *down* thanks to a built-in online discount.

- Once you get to the booking stage, you will also find the Optional extras, which can add further to the cost.

- In this instance you might like to book extra leg-room seats or just pre-bookable seats, while you will probably want to book your resort (taxi) transfers.

- After checking the necessary boxes, click on **Recalculate quote** (notice that the site changes to an https address, indicating it is a secure site for payment, with the padlock symbol appearing next to the Address bar).

- Your new total package price now appears.

- Click **Continue** to go to the payment stage.

- Double-check all the details are still correct.

- Complete the payment form and click **Confirm booking**.

- Remember to print out your booking confirmation.

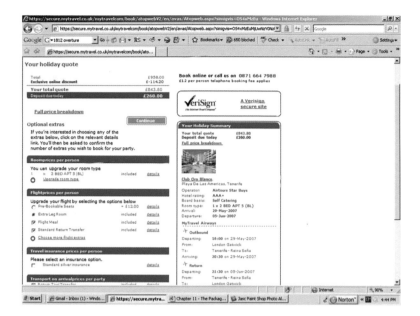

Don't worry **about quick decisions**

Take your time when making the decision to book your package. The worst thing that will happen is that you might occasionally 'time out' and have to go back to the beginning. Better that than to rush and book the wrong thing. Double-check your spelling when inputting your details and don't click **Book It** until you are entirely satisfied.

Searching by destination

If you are looking purely by destination (the most common kind of search), this is the time to put all your new-found searching skills into operation and make the internet work for you, remembering that the same package can have different prices with different online vendors. That means it is essential to shop around.

• Start by visiting one of the online travel agents' websites and clicking on the **Holidays** tab.

- Click on the **world map** or **destinations** list.

- Once you find a package that interests you, look for the actual operator of the holiday (you may need to click on the **More Info** link).

- If you can't find the actual operator of the holiday, try another package option or website.

- Go to the operator's own website and search for that package to find out the full brochure price.

For example – say you find a week's holiday to Corfu with Expedia and the actual operator of the package is Manos Holidays (if you don't know the address of their website, type Manos Holidays in your trusty search engine and you will quickly find **www.manos.co.uk**).

- Go to the Manos home page and type in the same details (i.e. for a week's holiday in Corfu).

- Find the identical package, and compare the *exact* final prices by clicking on the **Get quote** button.

Don't worry **about clicking Get Quote**

Never be afraid to click the **Get Quote** button. This does *not* commit you to booking anything, it merely ascertains the exact price for the package/flight/car hire you are looking at. You usually need to go through this process to get to the final price, as some include additional supplements or occasional discounts.

- Once you have made your travel agent versus tour operator comparison, decide who is cheaper.

- If the tour operator has the best price, you can be fairly sure they are the ones to book with.

- If the travel agent is cheaper, you may want to do one final check to see if anyone else can beat their price.

- Go to one of the aggregator or comparison websites (**www.travelsupermarket.com** is good for package holidays) and type in the same search details. This will search multiple online agents at once and give you a good final check of the options.

Searching by last-minute deals

If you are fortunate enough to be able to take advantage of late deals by going at short notice, you can again make good use of the internet.

- Visit a handful of the travel agent websites and simply check their Late Deals sections (also called Specials, Late availability etc).

- Check Teletext for late offers, as many tour operators use this as a 'bargain bin' for various deals. Go to **www.teletextholidays.co.uk** and click on the **Late Deals** link.

- This takes you to an extensive section of late deals and you can just select from the list that comes up or by departure region.

- Alternatively visit Bargain Holidays (**www.bargain holidays.com**) and check out their **Get away this weekend** link for some great last-minute packages.

- This provides packages leaving over the next two weekends, and you just need to choose which day you wish to search for late deals.

Pay special attention

When booking last-minute deals, part of the cost may be in 'hidden' non-optional supplements for things like peak-time flights and airport transfers. Be sure to look at the bottom-line figure to ascertain if it is a genuine saving on the regular price.

Your reminder box

- Use a website's Holidays section when searching for packages.

- Look for e-mail alerts on the websites that give you early notice of good deals and holiday sales.

- Pay close attention to the little 'extras' when pricing your package.

- Always double- and triple-check the booking details to confirm they are what you want *before* clicking the **Payment** button.

- Don't be afraid to get quotes from different sites. These don't commit you to booking.

- Use travel agent and aggregator websites to compare prices for the same package.

- Check the Last-Minute Deals sections for all the late bargains if you can travel at short notice.

Chapter 11

Transport

Once you have decided you are happy to take the DIY route rather than book a package (Chapter 10), you need to focus on the individual elements of your trip, starting with your actual transportation requirements.

This means finding flights and/or car hire, booking train tickets, ferries and even cruises. Each one has different requirements, and you usually need to combine several of them to form your DIY holiday.

The key here is to co-ordinate each one with your dates and travel requirements, along with your accommodation (which we cover in Chapter 12). For example, if you book a flight from London to Barcelona for a weekend break and need to hire a car for your arrival, you will need your flight details and timings when you go to book your car.

Booking flights

Booking an expensive travel item like a flight might seem daunting to start with, but it is no more complicated than ordering your shopping online. The terminology is different but the basics are the same: be sure of your requirements and read the details carefully before hitting the Payment button.

The main details to pay attention to are:

- Whether you need a Return, One-way or Multi-city ('open-jaw') flight.
- Your departure airport and destination city.
- Your travel dates (giving a date range if possible).
- The number and age of people travelling (some sites list 65+ as an option).

- If you have an airline preference (we suggest No for the best search results).

- The class of cabin you require (whether Economy, Business or First Class).

- Whether you want direct flights only. If you don't select this option, you may find some cheaper alternatives (especially on longer haul flights) by having one stop en route.

- And, on some occasions, if you need a ticket that is fully refundable (some low-cost airlines have serious refund limitations, which are part of their low-cost approach).

Pay special attention

When using one of the low-cost airlines, be sure exactly what destination airport they use, as some of them are smaller, less common airports away from city centres. For example, some airlines use Beauvais in France but still list it as 'Paris', even though it is 60km (37 miles) north of the city itself.

With the low-cost airlines, it is nearly always better to book as far in advance as possible, as their lowest fares are usually offered on a first come, first served basis.

Some even have low-fare sales many months in advance that can provide great deals, if you can book that far ahead and within specific requirements, e.g. flying midweek rather than at a weekend. Flights on a Friday and Saturday are nearly always more expensive than other days.

You can also be more prepared in advance thanks to the internet by researching your destination airport for things like baggage retrieval, where to find buses, taxis and the car hire offices and even the local weather.

- Say you are flying to Genoa. Go to your search engine and enter Genoa Airport.

- The top results will almost certainly turn up the official website for the airport.

- Click on the most official looking result (even if it is not in English).

- If the webpage comes up in the local language, look for the Union Jack symbol for the English version. Failing that, go back to the search results and click on the **[Translate this page]** option.

- Once you have the site in English, you can look up any details of interest.

More information

Want to find the best seats for your flight, or perhaps who has a good airline lounge? Skytrax is an aviation advice company with a wealth of information on their website, including passenger forums and rankings of all the airlines and airports, as well as good additional airport information.

- Go to **www.airlinequality.com**.

- For discussion forums, click on the **Passenger Opinions** tab and select your airline from the alphabetical list.

Good words to know

APD (or Air Passenger Duty): The government tax, per person, on all flights leaving from the UK.

Business class: An enhanced level of comfort and service in a separate cabin within the aircraft.

Economy: The basic (and cheapest) level of cabin accommodation on a flight. Some airlines try to fudge the issue by giving the economy cabin a fancy name, like World Traveller with British Airways.

First class: The top level of comfort and service, usually completely separate from the rest of the aircraft.

Fuel surcharge: An extra fee that airlines occasionally charge to cover increased fuel costs.

Premium economy: An enhanced version, usually with extra legroom (or World Traveller Plus).

Seat pitch: The legroom between seats e.g. a 32-inch seat pitch provides 32 inches from the edge of the seat to the back of the seat in front. In economy, 30–32 inches is standard.

- For a guide to the best seats, use the **Seating** tab.
- For ratings on every airline, click on **Airline Ranking**.

Getting the best price

We recommend the following steps to ascertain a range of quotes:

- Step 1: If you know which airline you want, try their home page first (if you don't know their web address, do a quick GoogleUK search for British Airways, EasyJet, or United Airlines, etc).

- Step 2: Get their standard price, then compare it by going to an online travel agent like Expedia.

- Step 3: Then use one of the comparison (aggregator) sites like TravelSupermarket or Sidestep to get another range of prices.

• Step 4: Finally, try bidding site Priceline as an example of somewhere that might have a bargain rate.

With three (or more) prices, you can be fairly confident you have found the best rate available at that time.

One final tip for unearthing bargain flights, especially on longer-haul routes like Florida, Sri Lanka and the Caribbean, is to book a package or fly-drive holiday with a tour operator and just use the flight part of the package.

Amazingly, these charter flight based packages can sometimes

Common mistakes

We asked one of the big online agents to tell us the typical mistakes people make when booking online.

Choosing sponsored results: Selecting from the list of Sponsored Links on a search engine rather than the genuine results from your search enquiry.

Not an airport!: You won't find great results for Flights to Benidorm or even Flights to Majorca; instead, you usually need to know the airport in each case for the best results, i.e. Alicante and Palma de Mallorca.

Spelling: The number one mistake is not spelling your destination or requirement properly.

Using the wrong search terms: Bargain flights won't produce many valid results, but using Cheap flights probably will.

Wrong airport: Many destinations have more than one airport. Make sure you find out which one you need in advance.

Wrong city: There is often more than one destination with the same name e.g. Birmingham (UK and USA), London (UK and Canada) and Sydney (Australia and Canada). Make sure you pick the right one when prompted during the booking process.

---

be cheaper than a scheduled air fare to places like Orlando, Colombo and Jamaica, and you can then arrange your own hotel and/or car hire.

If, for example, you are looking for a flight to Florida and the scheduled airfares are £300 or more, you might find a two-week package to Orlando (off peak) for less and simply forget about the accommodation part of the package so you can travel around on your own.

To do this, you would need to look for a package either with one of the online travel agents or direct with the tour operator.

Booking with an airline

If you book direct with an airline, you will find that nearly all use a straightforward form on the left-hand side of their home page, asking for all the basic details and offering you a price quickly. The British Airways site is a good example.

The key points to be familiar with are:

• How each airline shows the circular Return or One-way box, which you need to click on to specify your preference (and how they show the alternative for Multi-city or 'open-jaw' flight options).

• How to specify exactly which airport you need if there is more than one per city. For example, if you are in the London area, you usually need to state which airport you require, although some give you the chance to use 'London all' if you can be flexible.

- How to either input travel dates yourself or click on the little calendar symbol to select the dates you require. This is where you can indicate if your dates are flexible, and by how much, which can help to reveal cheaper flights.

- How tickets are usually shown as Economy in the first instance, and you must actively change it yourself, using a drop-down menu, if you want a different class of ticket.

- Finally, after you click on **Search** or **Get Flights**, be sure to double-check that the search results meet your requirements *before* going to the booking stage.

Don't worry about airport codes

Every airport has its own unique three-letter code, which identifies it for travel purposes, but you don't need to use this when booking a flight. For example, Heathrow is LHR, Gatwick is LGW and New York's John F Kennedy airport is JFK. Just make sure you type in your destination airport correctly, e.g. Montreal, Madrid, Prague, etc, and make sure it is the one you want when you click **Search**. That way you won't book a flight to London, Ontario, instead of London, UK!

Booking with an online agent

If you book with one of the online agents or aggregators, the process is similar, but you will have more results to consider.

The first thing to do with the online travel agents is make sure you are on the Flights part of their website. There will usually be a series of tabs along the home page (Home, Flights, Hotels, Car Hire, Holidays, Insurance, etc.). Click on **Flights**, then follow the procedure as laid down above for 'Booking with an airline'.

The only other difference you might find is that some sites will ask you for a Preferred Airline. Leave this blank if you want the best spread of results.

Don't worry **about airline 'alliances'**

You may come across airlines referring to their 'Alliance' partners, but this is strictly technical speak for airlines that agree to carry each other's passengers. This is really only of relevance if you have an Air Miles account with one airline which qualifies you for miles with one of its partners.

Pay special attention

The UK government's hefty Air Passenger Duty (a tax to fly from a UK airport) was doubled from February 2007, which means all departures to European destinations now cost £10 per person (£20 in Business Class or above) and those outside Europe are £40 (and £80). Other taxes and fees also apply to every booking, which means the first figure you are quoted online may not be the final cost. Some airlines (notably Ryanair and Aer Lingus) charge even to carry your luggage, which obviously adds another fee. All agents and online booking services are under pressure to include these 'extras' in their main quote in future, but you need to keep an eye on the bottom line.

Booking a charter flight

All the above online agents and booking systems handle only scheduled and low-cost flights. They do not search for charter flights, as these are a specialised area usually reserved for tour operator packages.

However, it is not uncommon for some of the charter airlines to sell flights direct to the consumer, and you can find some bargains here.

FlightsDirect is adept at searching out low-cost *and* charter airlines. So, if the cost with a scheduled airline or on one of the travel agent sites seems too high, try your flight search again on **www.flightsdirect.com**.

You can also search the charter airlines themselves, as some of their longer haul flights (notably to America and the Caribbean) are sold *only* on their own websites. The ones to look for are:

- **www.firstchoice.co.uk/flights/** First Choice Airways: to Europe, Africa, Florida, Jamaica and Sri Lanka.

- **www.flyastraeus.com** Astraeus: to Africa, Europe and America.

- **www.flythomascook.com** Thomas Cook Airlines: to Europe, Africa, India, Sri Lanka, Canada, Florida, Caribbean and Mexico.

- **www.monarchcharter.com** Monarch Airlines: to Europe, Florida, Kenya, Mexico and India.

- **www.mytravel.com** (and click on the Flights tab) MyTravel Airways: to Europe, Caribbean, America, Canada and Africa.

- **www.thomsonfly.com** Thomsonfly: to Europe, Middle East, Africa, Brazil, Florida, Mexico, India, Maldives, Thailand and Australia.

- **www.xl.com** XL Airways: to Europe, Caribbean, Africa and Florida.

Booking airport parking

The other thing you might need to do after booking your flights is to arrange airport parking, and this can easily be done online, too.

Generally speaking, there is always an online discount for booking in advance, whether you go directly to the airport's own parking site or use one of the many online car park booking agents.

You should also see how the two compare, so start by finding out about the airport's own parking arrangements.

- If you are flying out of Birmingham, find their home page by doing a quick search for Birmingham Airport.

- Look for the airport's official website, in this case **www.bhx.co.uk**.

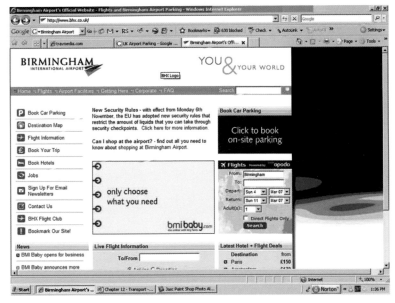

- On their home page, click the **Book Car Parking** link.

- Click **Book on-site car parking with NCP.**

- A new window will open, taking you to the on-site NCP car park booking page.

- Enter your details – date of departure, time you will arrive at the airport, return date and time and number of passengers, then click **Continue**.

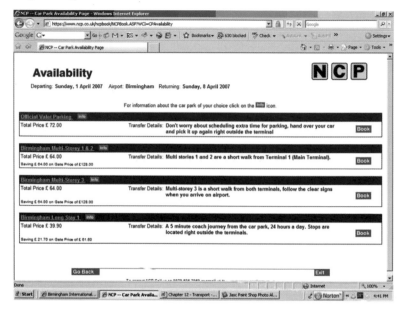

- Choose from the range of options and click **Book**.

- Fill in your customer and vehicle details and click **Continue**.

- Enter your credit card payment details and click **Continue**.

- Print out your booking confirmation.

Alternatively, you may like to arrange your car park booking through one of the many online booking agencies (including the online travel agents).

- A quick search for UK airport parking will bring up several dozen companies. You could also try specialist Airport Parking and Hotels at **www.aph.com**.

- Enter your parking requirements and click **Get a quote**.

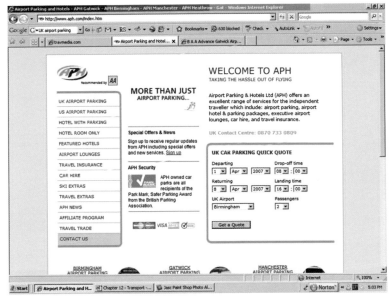

- The price for the NCP on-airport parking is the same, but you are also offered a cheaper alternative off-airport, so you can decide if you'd like to save some money in return for a longer transfer to the airport.

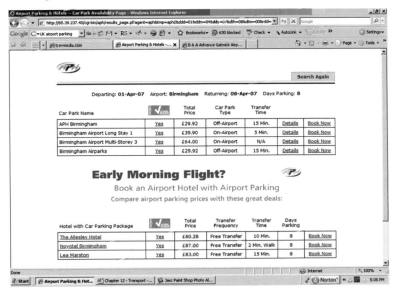

Some other airport parking sites you might like to try:

- **www.holidayextras.co.uk**
- **www.parkbcp.co.uk**
- **www.parking4less.co.uk**
- **www.purpleparking.com**

Pay special attention

Check whether your airport parking is on-site (i.e. within a short distance of the airport) or off-site (and requiring a longer bus transfer). Make a note of the transfer time from the car park to your terminal and allow yourself time to get parked and still be at the airline check-in desk in good time for your flight.

Booking car hire

When it comes to booking the car hire (or car rental, as it is referred to in some countries) part of your DIY holiday, the requirements are similar to flights.

The main details to pay attention to are:

- Your exact arrival airport (where there is more than one per city, for example, Orlando has both Orlando International and Orlando Sanford airports, and the car hire services would be different at each one).

- Your arrival date and, more importantly, the flight arrival and departure times (the Pick-up and Return times).

- The Category of car you require.

- What level of insurance you need (see pages 87–88).

- If you require more than one driver (as there is usually an Additional Driver fee).

- If there are any mileage restrictions.

- Booking in advance. This is nearly always cheaper, as most of the UK companies offer valuable all-inclusive polices and discounts for online advance bookings.

When it comes to booking, there are the car hire companies themselves and the agents that also sell car hire.

The former include the likes of Hertz, National, easyCar, Avis, Sixt, Europcar, Enterprise, Advantage, Thrifty, Budget, Alamo and Dollar (the latter two of which are the biggest for tourist business in the USA, the world's largest car hire market).

Good words to know

Most car hire companies use a similar range of terms for their car categories, which basically increase in size from **Economy** (or **Sub-compact**) and **Compact** through **Mid-Size** (or **Intermediate**) and **Full-Size** to **Luxury** (or **Premium**) and **Mini-Van**. Other terms include:

Convertible: A soft-top car with fold-away roof.

Speciality (or 'Specialty' in the USA): Usually a sports car or something unusual like a Hummer.

SUV: Sport Utility Vehicle (a 4 x 4 vehicle).

A Mid-Size will usually accommodate a family of four fairly comfortably, but four adults (and their luggage) would probably need a Full-Size.

You will also find some smaller, local companies at many airports, hence it is usually wise to start your search by looking up your destination airport's website for the options.

- Say you are flying to Orlando in Florida. Do a search for Orlando Airport and you will quickly find **www.orlando airports.net/goaa**.

- Go to the official website and look for their ground transportation arrangements (under Transport, Rental Cars or Car Hire). You will quickly find six companies 'on-airport' (i.e. available directly from the arrival terminal) and another 18 or so 'off-airport' (which you access by shuttle bus to their depot nearby).

- As well as all the companies listed above, you will find numerous smaller ones, including one called L&M Car Rental. Click on their direct link (in blue) and you will go to their website in a new browser window.

- Get a quote by entering your requirements in the Express Rates section.

- Note that this quote does not include any of the essential insurances you need to hire a car abroad, hence there will be extra to pay when you pick up your vehicle.

Once you have an idea of price from a local source, get a second quote from one of the main companies that has a UK booking site, like Alamo.

- Go to their home page at **www.alamo.co.uk**.

- Enter your car hire requirements in the Book car hire online section and click **Search**.

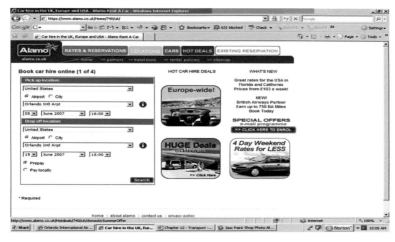

- Select your vehicle size and the level of coverage.

- Enter any additional equipment requirements, flight information, driver details, optional insurance upgrade (from Fully Inclusive to Gold, which includes extra drivers and fuel) and payment details.

- Note any additional fees and make a note of the final price.

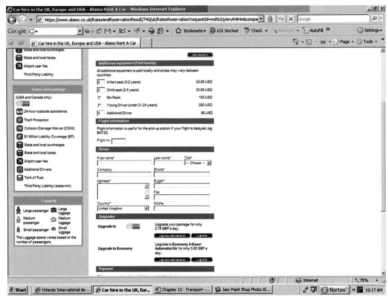

With two quotes under your belt, get a third, either from another rental company or one of the specific car hire specialists. These include Holiday Autos, Holiday Extras, Car Hire 3000, HireCars.co.uk and Auto Europe.

Or you can try the usual range of travel agents (Expedia, Travelcare, Opodo, etc) or one of the car hire aggregators like TravelSupermarket, Kelkoo and CarRentals.co.uk. The latter gets our vote in this instance.

- Go to their home page at **www.carrentals.co.uk**.

- Enter your car hire requirements (NB: the driver age requirement is important only if you are under 25!).

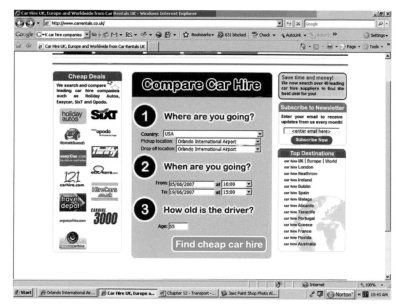

- You will immediately notice the results come up from *different companies* this time, as CarRentals.co.uk search a broad range of sources.

- Click on **Book Now** for the quote you like best.

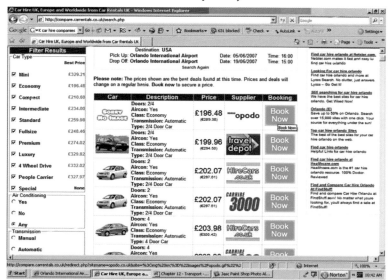

- If you choose the cheapest, which was from Opodo, you will be taken to the Opodo quote in a new browser window.
- Click on **Select** for the quote you are interested in.
- Check the details are still correct and click **Add to basket**.

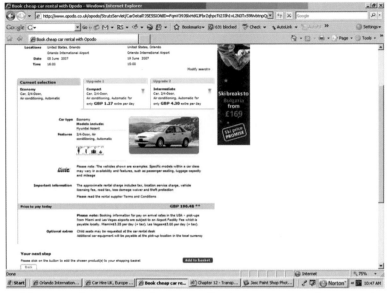

- You now have a good range of price quotes and can make your decision accordingly.
- If you are happy to stick with the Opodo quote, click on **Checkout** to complete the booking and payment form.

Other car hire companies and booking sites to consider:

- **www.avis.co.uk**
- **www.carhire3000.com**
- **www.easycar.com**
- **www.hertz.co.uk**
- **www.holidayautos.co.uk**
- **www.thrifty.co.uk**

Booking rail travel

With fewer sites offering rail travel, your choices are rather narrower. However, as mentioned in Chapter 6, you also have to negotiate the horrible complexity of British train fares.

Therefore, the main details to pay attention to are:

- Booking in advance (and online). This is usually the secret to getting the best deals as most UK timetables are issued 12 weeks in advance, when any cheap fares are usually posted.

- Use a Senior Railcard where at all possible. They cost just £20 for anyone over 60 and save a third off most fares (but not some peak journeys).

- Travel outside the main peak times (after 10am in most places) when possible.

- Check for Saver Singles fares as two singles can often be cheaper than a return.

UK rail

For travel within Britain, there are three main choices for booking:

- The Trainline (or **www.thetrainline.com**): A fully independent rail specialist with easy-booking facility, also offering travel around Europe and further afield. To buy online, you need to register with them first by providing your e-mail address and a password. They also charge a credit card fee per booking and automatically include insurance unless you uncheck the appropriate box.

- National Rail (**www.nationalrail.co.uk**): The UK's main information source, with terrific journey-planning information. You don't buy from them directly but are directed to the booking pages for the relevant train company (e.g. Virgin Trains and GNER), so it is a longer and more convoluted process.

- The train companies themselves, although, with 24 to

negotiate, unless you have a relatively simple journey (like the Eurostar to Paris), you are better off sticking with one of the above.

Good words to know

Class: Either Standard or First.

Eurostar: The high-speed passenger service direct from London, via Ashford in Kent, to Paris, Brussels, Lille, Disneyland Paris and the French Alps (seasonally).

Euro Tunnel: The car and freight service under the Channel from Folkestone in Kent to Calais in France.

FastTicket: An automated machine at many train stations for pre-booked tickets. Just swipe your credit card and enter the reference number (from your booking), and the tickets are dispensed.

Open Return: A return ticket without a specified return date.

Say you want to find fare and times for a journey from Brighton to Blackpool, with an overnight stay.

• Go to **www.thetrainline.com** and enter your journey details in their Quick Timetable.

• Click **Get times**.

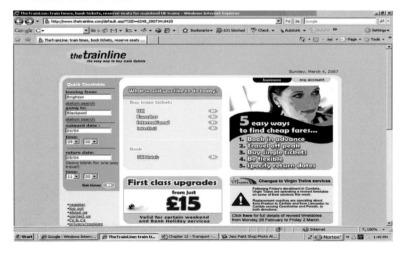

- Check availability and pricing by entering the passenger details, whether you have a railcard, if you want to travel via or *avoid* a particular station (leave blank if unsure), and the type of journey (Return, Open Return or Single).

- If you want more selections, click on **Find earlier trains** or **Find later trains**.

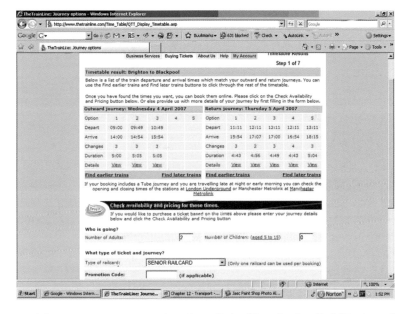

- After entering your details, click **Check Availability and Prices**.

- On your first visit, this is the point when you will need to register. So click the **arrow symbol** beside the words 'Register as a new user' and fill in your details – including your e-mail address and a password. If you are already a registered user, you will move automatically to the next stage.

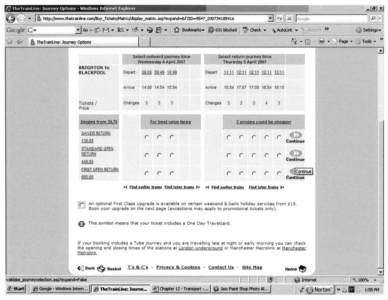

- The big advantage with Trainline is that it searches by both Return and two Single fares, the latter of which can sometimes be cheaper.

- You can check the Single fares by clicking on the line that says **2 singles could be cheaper**.

- Under the outward journey section, click on the circular window for your chosen time and do the same for the return journey.

- Click **Continue**.

- The next stage shows the journey details, lets you state a Seating preference, provides a box to 'name' your journey (if you want to save the details and find it later) and offers optional hotels and insurance (remember to uncheck the insurance boxes unless you actually want it).

- Click **Continue**.

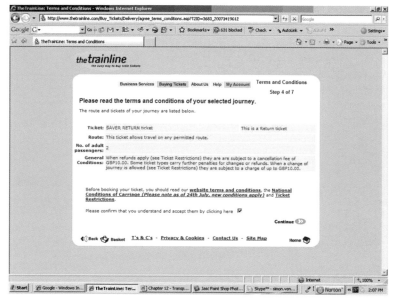

- Read the terms and conditions of the booking and click on the small square box that says you accept the terms and conditions.

- Click **Continue**.

- The next stage asks how you would like your tickets delivered, with a choice of (free) First class mail, FastTicket collection at your departure station, Next Day special delivery (£6 extra) or Same Day delivery (£10).

- Click **Continue**.

- You will then be asked to enter your Registered user details (e-mail and password). Then click the line that says **Log in to your account**.

- Check your Billing and Delivery address and click **Continue**.

- Check the journey details are still correct, the total ticket cost and click **Continue to payment**.

- Enter your credit card details and click **Buy ticket**.

- Print out your booking confirmation.

Other rail company websites:

- www.arrivatrainswales.co.uk
- www.centraltrains.co.uk
- www.firstgreatwestern.co.uk
- www.firstscotrail.com
- www.gner.co.uk
- www.northernrail.org
- www.southeasternrailway.co.uk
- www.southwesttrains.co.uk
- www.virgintrains.co.uk

Worldwide rail

For travel in Europe and beyond, a similar process applies with www.internationaltrainline.com, while there are also two other specialist booking companies:

- Rail Europe (or **www.raileurope.co.uk**): who sell tickets for a wide range of European services, including Eurostar, the French TGV trains and other high-speed services.

- Great Rail (or **www.greatrail.com**): for a huge range of journeys worldwide, including Scandinavia, Eastern Europe, Italy, Greece, South Africa, India, Japan, the USA and Canada, and even the Trans-Siberian Express.

Eurostar

It is worth making a note of what we believe is one of the best rail services in Europe as, for ease of use and value for money, Eurostar's services from London to France and Belgium take some beating.

It is a fast, reliable and comfortable way to travel, often cheaper and more efficient than flying – especially if you live in the south-east – and it is the perfect choice for short-break holidays to Paris, Lille, Brussels and Avignon.

Eurostar features easy car parking, good special needs help (including special fares for wheelchair users and easy access), simple luggage arrangements, business lounges, senior fares for the over 60s and even wireless internet access.

The new terminal at St Pancras International in London is also truly state of the art.

Their website (**www.eurostar.com**) includes a lot of useful information on their destinations, an Availability Calendar that shows all their cheapest fares (especially useful for early bookers), an online video tour and a range of weekend breaks including hotels.

To book, the main details to pay attention to are:

• Which class of ticket you require. Eurostar offers: Standard (which includes a guaranteed seat in their spacious, air-conditioned carriages – some with tables – onboard bar-buffet and a 30-minute check-in); Leisure Select (a larger, more comfortable seat, with champagne and a three-course meal served at your seat); and Business Premier (with additional fast-track check-in, fine food and wines and access to the business lounges).

- How flexible you need your ticket to be. Each Class is broken down into Fully Flexible (fully exchangeable and refundable, with no restrictions), Semi-Flexible (exchangeable for a fixed fee, non-refundable, and must include a Saturday night stay) and Non-Flexible (non-exchangeable, non-refundable and must include a Saturday night stay).

- There are also Standard Senior tickets, which are non-refundable and non-exchangeable.

You can search either by destination and date (on the left of their home page), or by their Budget Fares feature.

- For the latter, click on the **Find Cheap Fares** link on the Eurostar home page at **www.eurostar.com**.

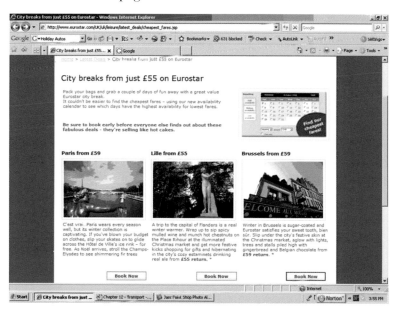

- Look at the options for Paris, Lille and Brussels.

- Decide which one you like and click **Book Now**.

- The monthly calendars show the full availability of their cheap fares (click on the **Next** link to go to the next month).

- Select your dates and click **Search**.

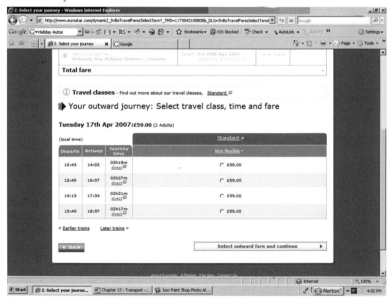

- The cheap fares offered are only Standard and Non-flexible, so if those don't appeal to you, return to the main booking page.

- Select your departure time and click on **Select outward fare and continue.**

- Do the same for the return time and fare.

- Check the fare. If you have previously registered with Eurostar, log in and continue; otherwise click on **Continue as guest.**

- Enter the Traveller details, seating preference (e.g. side by side) and ticket delivery method – either collect at station, by regular mail (free) or special delivery (£5).

- Click **Continue.**

- Review the booking details, click in the box to agree to Eurostar's Terms & Conditions and click **Continue to payment.**

- Enter your payment and address details and click **Continue.**

- Print out your booking confirmation.

Euro Tunnel

The final word on rail travel goes to the channel-crossing service of Euro Tunnel, which features a 35-minute drive-on rail service from Folkestone to Calais up to four times an hour at peak periods.

Their website offers various short-break options, plus an excellent Route planner feature (under the Travelling abroad link). LPG vehicles are not permitted on Euro Tunnel, though.

The main details to pay attention to are:

- Book at least a month in advance for the best fares.

- Choose from four different ticket types: a Standard fare (buy as a single leg or buy two singles for a return for any length of stay at set times); Flexi-plus (just turn up and go, plus lounge facilities and priority booking); Short-stay Saver (a saving of up to half the Standard fare if you stay away up to five days); and a Day/Overnight Fare (with the option to extend a stay for up to two days).

- You pay by car, not by passenger.

- To book, start by going to their home page at **www.euro tunnel.com** and click on **Passenger Travel**.

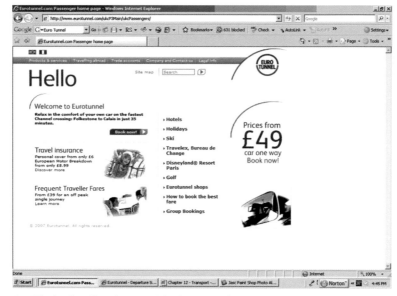

- Click the **Book now!** link (in red).

- Enter your journey dates, vehicle and country of origin and click **Continue**.

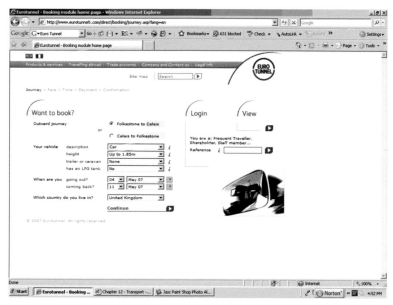

- Select preferred time and fare type.
- Click **Continue**.

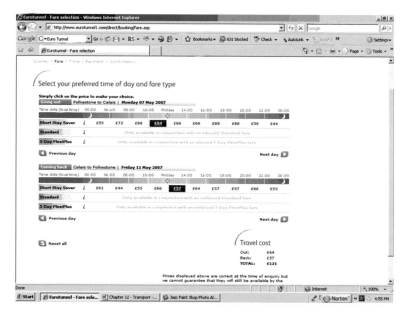

- Select your exact departure time.
- Indicate whether you would like insurance or not.
- Click **Continue.**
- Check the travel details, enter your own personal details, payment details and click **Make booking.**
- Print out your booking confirmation.

Booking ferries and cruises

Ferry and cruise bookings are more complicated and require more careful consideration, although that shouldn't stop you seeking out the great value and bargains to be had in this sphere as well.

The two are distinctly different, although some longer ferry journeys try to pass themselves off as mini-cruises. A ferry is primarily a means of transport to Ireland or mainland Europe, while a cruise is a holiday in itself.

Ferry travel

Booking a ferry crossing is a similar process to rail travel, and notably the Euro Tunnel service (one of the cross-Channel route's biggest competitors).

The main details to note are:

- What route do you need? There are at least a dozen routes to France, seven to Ireland, three to the Channel Islands and Holland, two to Spain and Norway, and one each to Sweden and Denmark.
- You are usually booking a time slot on a ferry, so you need to arrive at least 30 minutes in advance.
- Do you require a cabin for the journey? On an overnight sailing it will probably be worthwhile, but for 5–6 hours you might manage without.

- Would you like to upgrade on board? Many operators offer 'extras' like an exclusive lounge, priority boarding and free tea, coffee and soft drinks.

Again, your choice is in booking direct with one of the 20 or so ferry companies or using a specialist online agent. If you start with the agent and then double-check by getting a quote from the ferry line, you should be sure you have a good price.

For a Dover-Calais trip (the UK's busiest route), try first with Seaview.

- Go to their home page at **www.seaview.co.uk/ferries.asp**.

- Under the heading Find Your Ferry, click on **By Route**.

- On the drop-down menu, select Dover–Calais (P&O) and enter the number of passengers.

- Click **Get Price**.

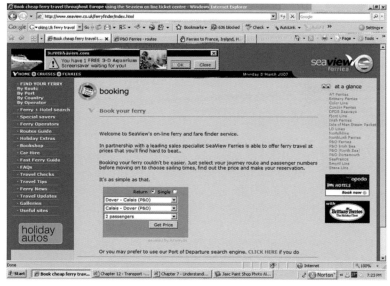

- Enter your travel dates and a time for each crossing.

- Enter the Passenger Ages and Method of Travel (Car).

- Click **Continue**.

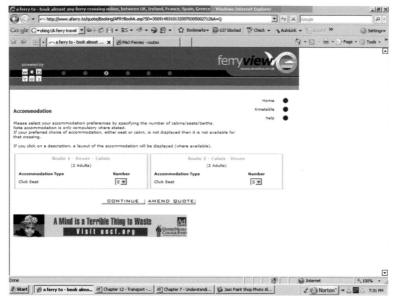

- The Accommodation requirement is an *option* if you would like P&O's extra Club seating upgrade. If you would like it on either crossing, enter the number of seats (2 in this example).

- Check the price and details. To continue, click on **Click Here To Book**.

- Enter your vehicle and passenger details and again click on **Click Here To Book**.

- Enter your credit card details and click on **Click Here To Book**.

- Print out your booking confirmation.

Unfortunately, there is no search engine that will give you comparative prices with a similar service on the same route.

So, to compare the P&O price with the SeaFrance service, you would have to repeat the steps above, only, on the drop-down menu, select Dover-Calais (SeaFrance).

Once you have chosen the ferry company, do a similar price search with them directly.

- Go to the P&O Ferries home page at **www.poferries.com**.

- Enter your travel details and click on **Book/Get Quote**.

- Check which outward sailing you require and click on **Select**.

- Do the same for the return journey and click **Select**.

- Select any options and upgrades (like the Club Lounge seats).

- Click on **Continue**.

At this stage you can see if the price quote is comparable and whether to continue with the online agent or the ferry company.

- To continue with P&O Ferries, enter your personal and vehicle details.

- Click **Continue.**

- Enter your credit card payment details.

- Click **Continue.**

- Print out your booking confirmation.

Other ferry company websites:

- **www.brittany-ferries.com** Brittany Ferries from Portsmouth, Poole and Plymouth to France and Spain.

- **www.dfds.co.uk** DFDS Seaways from Harwich and Newcastle to Denmark, Holland and Sweden.

- **www.ferrycrossings-uk.co.uk** Ferry Crossings-UK, a general booking website.

- **www.ferryto.co.uk** Cross Channel Discount Ferry Crossings general booking website.

- **www.poferries.com** P&O Ferries from Dover to Calais, Portsmouth to Spain and Hull to Rotterdam and Zeebrugge.

- **www.poirishsea.com** P&O Irish Sea from Liverpool to Dublin, Cairnryan and Troon to Larne, and Rosslare to Cherbourg.

- **www.seafrance.com** SeaFrance from Dover to Calais.

- **www.stenaline.co.uk** Stena Line from Harwich to Hook of Holland, Fishguard to Rosslare (Ireland), Holyhead to Dun Laoghaire and Dublin (Ireland), Fleetwood to Larne (Northern Ireland), Stranraer to Belfast, and Denmark to Norway and Sweden.

More information: The Met Office issues regular weather forecasts for the shipping lanes, and you may like to look up the forecast for your route on **www.metoffice.gov.uk/weather/marine/**.

Cruises

The main requirement here is to take more time to do your 'homework', as advised in Chapter 6. There are some fabulous websites for great background reading, and you should start here before venturing to make a booking.

A cruise makes a great choice as it is full board (and usually as much as you can eat!), the scenery changes on a daily basis (and you need to unpack just once), you visit numerous interesting ports of call and there is a wide and varied range of onboard entertainment.

Put simply, you travel in style and eat very well and often for a fraction of the cost you would pay for a similar itinerary (and accommodation) on land.

The UK's Passenger Shipping Association (PSA) is at the forefront of providing invaluable independent advice, and you can look up their website at **www.discover-cruises.co.uk**.

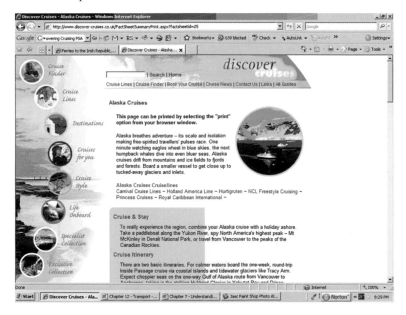

Bear in mind that virtually every cruise line declares itself luxury this and luxury that. Many publications publish accepted star rating guides to the cruise lines and their ships, and you should consult one of these for the independent verdict:

- **www.fodors.com** (click on the **Cruises** tab).
- **www.worldofcruisingmagazine.com/planner.php**.

Once you are ready to book, you should find one of Britain's specialist cruise agents, who can all offer extra advice with your booking.

- Visit the PSA's website of accredited cruise agents at **www.psa-psara.org**.
- Click on the **Consumers** link, and you will get a full list of all the 165-plus cruise agents.
- Many of them have websites you can peruse for general information before booking.
- The travel agent MyTravel also have a specialist agency called The Cruise Store at **www.thecruisestore.co.uk**.

Good words to know

Balcony cabin: Cabin with its own private veranda.

Inside cabin: Internal cabin with no external window or sea view.

Outside cabin: Cabin with a sea view.

Stateroom: Fancy term for cabin!

Suite: A genuinely fancy cabin (with extra living room and enhanced amenities).

However, even big sites like The Cruise Store are unable to book everything online, so you may need to find what you are interested in online, then call the agent concerned.

Remember the four basic rules before you book:

• Decide where you want to cruise.

• Work out the right cruise line for you.

• Decide when you want to go.

• If you don't want to fly, there are various options from UK ports.

A typical agent is Sussex specialist The Cruise Line Ltd. Look them up at **www.cruiseline.co.uk**.

• On their home page, go to their Cruise Finder and enter your range of dates, the cruise region that interests you (say, the Mediterranean), leave the Duration, Shipping Line and Ship lines as optional.

• Click **Search**.

From the long list of results, click on the individual results that interest you. However, to book, you need to submit an online form to the agency, and they will then contact you to discuss details.

Most agents work on this basis, as the list of variables for a cruise is often too long to be workable online.

Finally, if you can wait until the last minute, you will often find some great late bargains, as long as you don't mind a limited choice of cabin.

Other cruise websites:

* www.cruisedirect.com
* www.cunard.com
* www.easycruise.com
* www.fredolsencruises.com
* www.islandcruises.com
* www.oceanvillageholidays.co.uk
* www.pocruises.com
* www.seaview.co.uk/cruises.asp

River cruises

River cruising is a small specialist area of cruising and encompasses everything from canal barging in Britain to luxury cruises on the Yangtze, Nile and even the Irrawaddy River in Burma/Myanmar.

The most popular areas are the Rhine/Danube rivers in central Europe, the French rivers of the Rhone, Saone and Seine and the Nile in Egypt.

Look up the following river cruise specialists:

* **www.deilmann.co.uk** Peter Deilmann Cruises run right across Europe, from France and Holland to Poland, Hungary and Bulgaria.

* **www.gobarging.com** European Waterways offer luxury barge holidays in Scotland, Ireland, England, France, Belgium, Holland, Germany, Czech Republic and Italy.

- **www.majesticamericaline.com** Delta Queen Steamboats can give you a trip back in time on period paddleboats on the Mississippi in America.

- **www.orient-express.com** Orient Express run luxury barge holidays in France and cruising on the Irrawaddy in Burma.

- **www.vikingcruises.co.uk** Viking River Cruises offer a full European choice, plus Russia and China.

More information

One general website which is worth looking at for a huge variety of ideas and tips is MoneySavingExpert.com, created by ultra-savvy journalist Martin Lewis.

If you don't already use it for other areas of finance (including banking, shopping and insurance), you should, while it also has specialist sections and up-to-the-minute advice on cheap flights, rail travel and much more.

- Just type in their address, www.moneysavingexpert.com.

- Click on the **Travel & Transport** link on the left-hand menu.

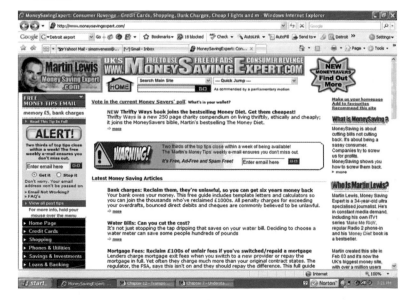

- Take your pick from a wide range of articles and advice, especially for flights, train tickets and even mobile phones.

- Check the **Forums** section for more direct input from fellow travellers.

One notable service from MoneySavingExpert is their amazing Flight Checker, which actually searches for flights with the low-cost airlines according to price rather than date.

The big advantage here is that it shows up the dates when the *real* bargain-basement fares are available, which aren't always obvious from searching an airline's own webpage (even though they may have 'Sale! Fares from £1!' all over the page).

- Go to the MSE home page and look down the left for the MoneySaving Tools section, and click on **FlightChecker**.

- Enter your departure airport and destination (it is not fully comprehensive, so some airports may not feature).

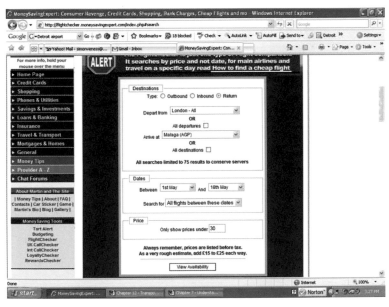

- Put in the range of dates you are interested in (say, for the first half of May for a flight to Malaga in Spain).

- Enter a low price that you think the rock-bottom rates might be at.
- Click **View Availability**.

If FlightChecker shows no results for your chosen destination, try increasing the price in £10 increments until you have some success (you need to add on £15–£25 each way to cover the taxes and APD, which FlightChecker is not able to include in its quote).

Congratulations – you have just made fantastic use of the internet!

Your reminder box

- Co-ordinate your individual DIY elements with each other so you don't end up with flights and a hotel booked for different dates.

- Look for advance sales with the low-cost airlines.

- Get three (or more) flight quotes by searching the airline's own website, an online travel agent and an aggregator website.

- Don't be afraid to book a package to some destinations if it comes up cheaper than a flight-only search.

- If scheduled flights seem too expensive, try one of the chartered airlines.

- Book airport parking online for the best deals.

- For car hire, ensure you have comprehensive insurance, and book in advance for the best all-inclusive deals.

- With rail travel, two single fares can sometimes be cheaper than a return.

- Don't forget Euro Tunnel as an alternative to the cross-Channel ferries.

- Do lots of online research on cruises before booking.

Chapter 12

Accommodation

Whether you are still in the research phase or ready to put your money on the table, making sure you have a comfortable place to stay should be right at the top of your To-Do list.

Along with any flight arrangements, accommodation is one of the most important decisions you will have to make, and these two elements should be considered simultaneously. Before you book a flight, you must know what sort of lodging is available in your desired destination and, before you book lodging, you must know if you can get there in the first place.

Chapter 11 helped you find the best deals on flights. Now we will sort out the various accommodation options, from camping to luxury resorts and everything in between.

Finding the best place to stay

A bewildering array of accommodation is available for the asking and we encourage you to think beyond the traditional choices of the past, when the standard hotel or B&B were your only lodging options. From the intimacy of a boutique resort to the all-inclusive benefits of hiring a private villa, the accommodation you choose can be every bit as exciting as the destination itself.

Choosing the right accommodation

The sort of holiday you are seeking will probably rule out some choices straight away. Solo travellers and couples may have different needs than those taking a family-reunion type of holiday. Before we search for a place to stay, let's review some options.

- Hotels are familiar to most travellers and remain the most popular choice.

- The intimacy of a Bed and Breakfast may appeal to solo guests or couples who enjoy a communal atmosphere, along with the privacy of their own room within their host's home.

- Caravanning or camping may be the right choice for more adventurous travellers.

- Villas and holiday homes are enjoying a surge in popularity for larger groups. They are essentially a private home, with two or more bedrooms, full kitchen facilities and a main living area.

- Home exchanges are another option, especially for long-term travel, though you must be open to having others stay in your home while you stay in theirs.

Don't worry about making a choice

It is easy to compare the benefits of various types of accommodation. Your skills using more than one browser window are all you need to do some comparison shopping, using one browser window to search for hotels, a second to search for villas and so on. You can quickly go back and forth between windows to compare prices, amenities and more.

Finding hotels and motels

To search for a specific hotel, motel or chain, visit their website directly or use an online agent. To find a hotel's own website:

- Type the hotel or motel name or the name of the chain ("Sheraton Park Tower" London or "Thistle Hotels") into a Google Search box.

- Press **Enter**.

To find a specific hotel or a variety of hotels for comparison shopping, use an online travel agent such as Expedia, Travelocity or Hotels.co.uk.

- Type www.expedia.co.uk into the Address bar.

- Press **Enter**.

- In the Create your trip box select Hotel only.
- Enter your requirements and click **Search**.

- Browse the list generated for accommodation in your chosen location.

We will explore direct purchase and online agents in greater depth later in this chapter.

Finding villas and holiday homes

Because many online holiday villa rental websites advertise only the homes in their inventory, the most efficient way to search for villas and holiday homes is to enter search terms for the area you will be visiting.

- Type "vacation villas", "holiday homes" or "villas" and your destination ("villas" Spain or "villas" Barcelona) into a Google Search box.

- Press **Enter**.

You can also use the same search terms, without including a destination, for websites that have an international inventory, though their locations and inventory may be limited. Let's practice by looking for a villa in Austria.

Pay special attention

When booking a villa, be certain you have the address, phone number of the owner or management company, directions, key collection details, and the e-mail address of the person you are booking with. Be sure to ask for a confirmation of deposit and always read the terms of use and what is included in your rental before booking.

• Type *"vacation villas"* into a Google Search box.

• Press **Enter**.

• Click on **Vacation Villas International**.

• Click on **Austria** under the heading Europe.

• Click on **Salzburg** on the map.

• Choose **Pinzgauer-Saalachtal** under the heading Holiday Homes in Salzburger Land.

• Browse the list of available villas, clicking on the title to view details and pictures.

More villa links:

- **www.holidaylettings.co.uk** 11,000 international vacation villa listings.

- **www.holiday-rentals.co.uk** 21,000 properties worldwide.

- **www.myvillarenters.com** Instant reservation confirmation is a big bonus here.

- **www.VRBO.com** Villa Rentals By Owner.

Bed and breakfast

Hospitality of the warmest kind is the order of the day, along with fresh, wholesome breakfasts, fascinating company and gracious hosts willing to share not only their local knowledge, but also their home. Bed and breakfasts can truly have the feel of a holiday spent in the company of friends, with as much privacy as each guest desires. Seniors may especially enjoy the intimacy of a B&B.

- Type "Bed and Breakfast" into a Google Search box.

- Press **Enter**.

- In this example, click on the link for **Bed and Breakfast Nationwide**.

- Scroll down the main page until you see a list of locations.

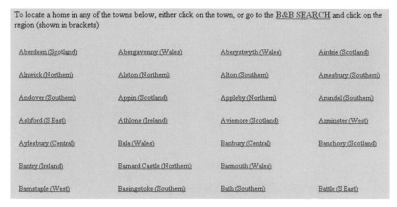

- Click on the link for **Bath (Southern)**.

- Browse the results list, clicking on **More Details** for accommodation details.

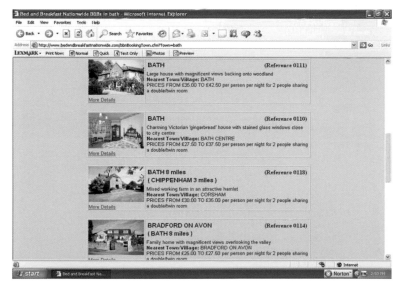

- While reading the details, look for a direct link to that B&B's website and for the owner's e-mail address.

- For choices further afield, try search terms such as "International Bed and Breakfasts", "Bed and Breakfasts" Toronto or simply "B&Bs".

- Always read the terms and conditions before booking.

More B&B links:

- **www.bnb-directory.com** Comprehensive directory of International B&Bs.

By now you can probably see a pattern in the process of searching. The step-by-step directions are similar, only the search terms will change.

Home exchanges

It isn't everyone's cup of tea, but home exchanges may be a good choice if you are looking for 'free' accommodation and are willing to let an exchange family use your home while you stay in theirs.

- Type "Home Exchange" into a Google Search box.

- Press **Enter**.

- Click on the link to **HomeExchange.com**.

- Use the drop-down menu on the main page to select a region.

- Select a location from the results list.

- Click on any exchange home links that appeal to you.

While you may be able to view the details for each location, home exchange websites often have a membership fee if you decide you would like to use their service or list your home. This helps ensure exchangers are serious when seeking offers for exchange.

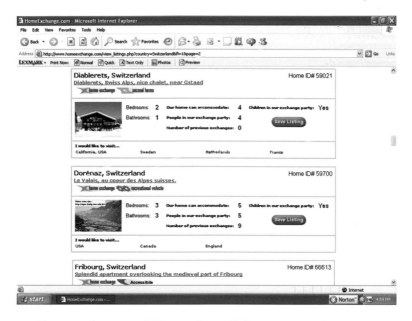

- Also try the term "Home Swap" for more results.

- Be sure to read the site's FAQ page for helpful suggestions before listing your home or when making or replying to an offer.

Don't worry about bills, cars or pets

Everything is negotiable when you do a home swap. Take several weeks if necessary to 'get to know' the other swap family and to make agreements regarding who will pay bills, whether or not you will swap cars, if pets will stay in the home or any other necessary details. One non-negotiable issue is insurance. Your homeowners insurance must include coverage while exchange guests are in residence. The same goes for your car insurance if you swap cars.

More home swap links:

- **www.homebasc-hols.com** Home Base Holidays.

- **www.ihen.com** International Home Exchange Network (they also have villa rentals).

Camping and caravanning

Adventurous holidaymakers seeking the great outdoors have their own set of needs, dependent largely upon whether or not they have all the equipment necessary for camping or a caravan expedition. A general search can be made using terms such as "Campsites Nevada" or "Campsites Europe".

- Type "UK campsites" into a Google Search box.

- Press **Enter**.

- Click on **The UK Camp Site for Tent and Caravan Campers in the UK** link.

- Overlook the rather garish background colour of the main page and, if you know the name of the campsite you would like to visit or want to narrow your search by town or county, enter the name into the Campsite Quick Search box on the main page.

- Follow the handy step-by-step directions to navigate the website, clicking on any campsite links that appeal to you.

Many websites will allow you to request specific campsite features, further narrowing your search. Look for an Advanced Search feature as you browse.

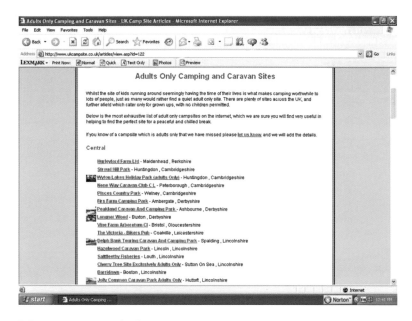

More campsite links:

- **www.camping.uk-directory.com** Camping and Caravanning UK (directory).

- **www.itravelnet.com/directories/camping.html** Worldwide campsites. Directory only.

- **www.thecampingandcaravanningsite.co.uk** Easily navigated site with UK destinations.

Unusual accommodation

If the idea of sleeping in a castle, a cave, a treehouse or an ice hut appeals to you, maybe you are ready to try something completely different in the way of lodging. The internet opens up a world of surprising choices when it comes to unusual accommodation, simply by inserting a few creative terms into a Search box.

Good word to know

Qualifier: A word or phrase that limits or modifies your search terms. Adding qualifier words such as rustic, novel or underwater to your search for hotels will yield results pertaining only to that particular type of accommodation.

Finding non-traditional lodging

- Search for specialised accommodation in general by using qualifiers such as: boutique, novel, unique, quirky or unusual. For example, "quirky accommodation" or "unique hotels".

- Search for a specific type of specialised hotel using terms such as "ice" hotels or "treehouse" accommodation. In this instance, putting only the qualifier in quotation marks will return better results than putting both terms in quotes. Essentially, you are telling the search engine to look for just "this kind" of accommodation.

Don't worry about search combinations

Your search will reap different results depending on whether you use the word hotel or accommodation, where you place quotation marks and which qualifier you use. Try different combinations. The descriptions under each search result will give you an idea of how successful the combination of terms and quotation marks has been and you can always try something different if you don't find what you're looking for the first time.

Your search will undoubtedly result in several useful websites, especially if you know exactly what sort of accommodation you are interested in trying. Before you have a go, let's look at a few possible results you may encounter as you search: a directory, a straightforward website and a link within a website.

Searching with a directory

If you prefer to use a directory rather than searching by terms, try somewhere like Search and Go. Remember, a directory narrows down your search as you click through a series of lists. However, they are often cumbersome to use and may produce limited results.

* Type www.searchandgo.com into the Address bar.

* Click on the **Travel** link in the right-hand column.

* Scroll down until you see the heading Section Menu in the right-hand column.

* Click on the **Travel Directory** link under that heading.

* Scroll down until you see the Categories heading.

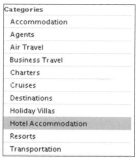

Categories
Accommodation
Agents
Air Travel
Business Travel
Charters
Cruises
Destinations
Holiday Villas
Hotel Accommodation
Resorts
Transportation

* Click on **Hotel Accommodation** under that heading.

* Click on **Unusual Accommodation** under the Categories heading.

* Browse the resulting options, clicking on any location title that appeals to you. You will be taken to their website for more details.

Unusual Hotels of the World

Most websites have a small section devoted to unique accommodation. Unusual Hotels of the World is an entire website devoted to lodging with a difference. It is easy to navigate, has 20 categories to choose from, loads of photos and a ratings system from 'different' to 'Wow'.

- Type **www.unusualhotelsoftheworld.com** into the Address bar and press **Enter**.

- The main page reveals 20 icons, which link you to various categories of novel accommodation.

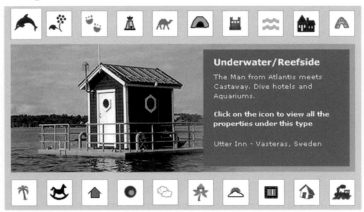

- Click once on an **icon** to generate a short description (such as Island, Lighthouses or Rainforest/Jungle/Bush) and a representative photo for that category.

In the example below, we see One-offs/Unclassified and the biggest Beagle in the world, which is really Dog Bark Park Inn. Now that's unique!

- Once you have clicked on any icon, you will be able to scroll your cursor over the remaining icons, without clicking on them, to generate the description and corresponding photo.

- To view accommodation options within a category, click on the appropriate icon twice.

- For more details on a particular resort, click on the **View More Details** box within that resort's description box.

- Scroll down the description page to view a small photo gallery for your chosen location.

Unusual accommodation links within general websites

Websites that include accommodation information in general may also have a section focused on unusual hotels. It may take some searching to find the link, so let's use the Enjoy England site for practice.

- Type www.enjoyengland.com into the Address bar.

- Click on the **Where to stay** tab at the top of the page.

- Click on the **Search for a place to stay** link under the Search Accommodation heading.

Search Accommodation | Quality Ratings

Where to stay

Search accommodation

We have over 27,000 places to stay across England from hotels to bed & breakfasts and cottages to caravans, camping and hostels. Every one has been visited by an independent VisitBritain or AA assessor and carries a star rating, so you can be sure of quality.

Search for a place to stay

- Click on the **Read about our accommodation types** link under the Accommodation types heading.

Accommodation types

Whatever your destination, budget or length of stay, there is a huge range of quality accommodation for you to choose from in England.

Read about our accommodation types

- Scroll down to the bottom of the page and click on the **More about unusual accommodation** link under the Unusual accommodation heading.

- Click on the **Read more about unusual accommodation** link. Notice underlined blue text within the main body of the text – these are active links to websites offering unique accommodation.

Quirky accommodation

Traditionally, England is renowned for its scenic countryside and historic city life, for its superb shopping and its relaxing spa breaks. A better-kept secret (but just as easy to discover is that England is peppered with a great variety of unusual places to stay. From a quirky town hotel to a storybook country hideaway, we've found a selection that is sure to stir the imagination...

If history is your passion, you could spend a weekend or longer self-catering at Pekes Manor in beautiful Sussex, whic tells a story dating back to William the Conqueror. You can stay in the Manor itself, which sleeps up to 18, or choose from one of the smaller properties on the grounds, including the Gate Cottage, and a traditional Oast House for which the area is famous.

Or if you'd prefer to be waited on in unusual surroundings, then perhaps Oxford's Malmaison would be more your style. A converted prison, it has retained many features, such as the original cells, door and bars. Whatever your crime, you're sure to enjoy doing time at this lovely boutique hotel.

For the more adventurous, you could try taking in England's dramatic coast in a traditional lighthouse. No longer operational, (so a good night's sleep is guaranteed), Cromer Lighthouse on the Norfolk coast offers

- Click on one of them to view the web page, which will pop up in a new browser window (remember, you can click on the red X in the upper right corner of the screen to close the new window).

Some websites will have a list of links rather than links within the body of text. Click on the links that appeal to you.

Don't worry about having to search

It may be a challenge finding an obscure link within a website, but it can be done and you might just find a hidden gem in the area where you wish to stay. The main thing is, don't give up. Even long-time internet users have to work hard to find what they want, at times.

More unique accommodation sites:

- **http://hotels.about.com/od/uniqueandunusualhotels** A directory with links to unusual accommodation, mostly within the United States. (NB: do not include www. in the address).

- **www.i-escape.com** Off the beaten track hideaways.

- **www.uniqueplacestostay.com.au** Australia and New Zealand.

- **www.whereintheworld.co.uk** Click on the **Room with a View** link on the left side of the main page.

Buying direct or through an online agent

Now that you are ready to make a reservation, let's look at options when it comes to comparing rooms and rates. In Chapter 5 we learned about the pros and cons of using online agents, tour operators or aggregators. Another option is to book directly, using the hotel's website. How do you know which method will produce the best deal?

Simple! Open two or more browser windows for instant comparison shopping. Remember, you can easily open an additional browser window by placing your curser over the link you wish to view and right-clicking on it, then clicking **Open in New Window**. If you are not following a link, double-click on the icon you use to connect to the internet.

Understanding inventories

It is important to understand how online agents obtain their inventory and how it affects your search. Agents such as Expedia purchase a number of rooms for each day, at discounted rates, then re-sell them near or below rack rate. When their inventory sells out, the website shows No Availability for that date and room type.

> **Good word to know**
>
> **Rack rate:** An accommodation's standard rate, without any discounts.

Different online agents will therefore have different inventories, depending on how many people use them to book a room for any given day. Expedia may have sold out but Travelocity may still show availability. Online agents may have no rooms when the hotel itself still shows availability. Checking three or more sources could reap positive results.

Using an online agent

Online agents allow you to search for a specific hotel or comparison shop among many hotels. In this example we will use Expedia. Remember, you must register as a member (which is free) to reserve a room.

- Type www.expedia.co.uk into the Address bar.

- Press **Enter.**

- Click on **Hotel only** in the Create your trip box.

- Fill in your destination (for this example use Dublin).

- Click on the **Check-in** and **Check-out** boxes, which will generate a calendar.

- Click on the appropriate date to enter your arrival and departure dates.

- Enter desired number of rooms and number of adults and children (if any) by clicking on the drop-down menu under each heading.

- Click on the **Search** button.

- You may be prompted to indicate the exact city you are visiting if there is more than one location by that name (e.g. Bath). Click on the correct location, then click **Continue**.

- You may see a section above the results list which allows you to narrow your search by vicinity (using a drop-down menu) or amenities. Adjust your search as needed, or browse the general list below it.

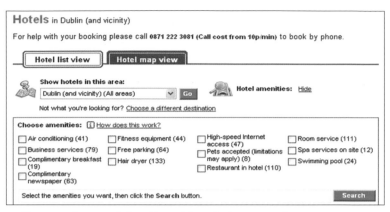

- Browse the resulting list of hotels in your chosen area.

- Click on the **More hotel info** link for any accommodation that interests you, for further details and photos.

- Within the next page, click on **See hotel information** or **See room information**.

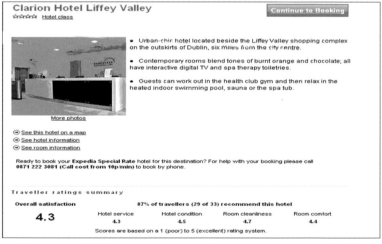

- If you would like to view more locations, click on the **Back to search results** link near the upper left corner of the page.

- When you are ready to book, click the **Continue to Booking** link within the hotel information page (or **Book It** if you are viewing the results list).

Continue to Booking

- Follow the step-by-step instructions, remembering to review details and read the rules and restrictions carefully.

- After you fill in your payment information, review your details to confirm they are correct before making the final purchase.

Always comparison shop using more than one online agent. By checking several well-known sites such as Travelocity (**www.travelocity.co.uk**), Hotels.com (**www.hotels.co.uk**), ebookers (**www.ebookers.co.uk**) and TravelSupermarket (**www.travelsupermarket.com**) you can be fairly certain you will find the best price.

Don't worry about omitting information

If you omit important information you will be prompted to enter it before you continue booking. Read the red text, which will tell you exactly what has been left out.

Pay special attention

When using an online agent always look for a tab or link titled Hot Deals (or similar). If your dates are flexible or a location is offering an internet-only discount, you may reap significant savings.

More useful online agents:

- **www.luxuryexplorer.com** Focused on luxury travel. No chain or big brand hotels.

- **www.sidestep.com** Compares several online agents for pricing, then links you to them for booking.

- **www.travelbag.co.uk** Hotels, car hire and flights.

- **www.travelres.co.uk** Focus on hotels worldwide.

Booking direct

A hotel website may offer Specials that are not available through an online agent or may be the only choice if you are finding No Availability through online agents. In this example we will use Hotel Cipriani in Venice.

- Type "Hotel Cipriani" Venice into a Google Search box.

- Click on the **Hotel Cipriani** link on the results page.

- You may be taken directly to the hotel website or given a selection of hotels within a brand. In this instance, click on the **Hotel Cipriani** link at the bottom of the page.

- Browse the website for more information or look for the Check Availability box, filling in your travel details.

- When you are ready to book a room, look for the **Book online** link (also Reservations or similar) and click on it.

- Fill in your travel details and click **Check availability**.

- Browse the list of room categories, clicking **Select** when you find the room you wish to book. You can always click the **Back** button to view more choices.

Deluxe Room with king bed

Deluxe rooms are elegantly decorated, overlooking the Hotel gardens, or lagoon (assigned on arrival) some include private balcony and jacuzzi, and are approximately 25 square metres in size.

Rate per night: €850.00 (USD 1104) Info

Select ⊖

- Fill in your Personal and Payment details and click **Complete reservation**.

Depending on the terms of booking, your credit card may be charged at that time. Be sure to review all details before completing your reservation.

Pay special attention

Regardless of how you book, make sure you know whether the price quoted is in sterling (GBP), US dollars, Euros or another currency.

Late offers and price bidding

Travellers with flexible dates stand to save a great deal of money through late offers and price bidding. Late offers can be found, usually under a link labelled Hot Offers, Last Minute Specials or similar, on the hotel website or online agent site and are booked in exactly the same way as you would book a room at regular rate.

Priceline is the pioneer in the bidding industry. Price bidding is much more complicated than direct booking, requiring flexibility in your travel dates, room requirements and location. If your bid is accepted, savings can be significant.

Late offers

Flexible dates are the key when taking advantage of late offers. Visit several online agents or hotel websites, such as ebookers (**www.ebookers.com**) or Expedia (**www.expedia.co.uk**).

- Click on the **Hotels** link on the main page when using an online agent.

- Look for the **Hot Deals** (Last Minute Deals or similar) link and click on it.

HOTEL HOT DEALS	
Prices are per room (sleeps 2) per night in GBP (Pounds Sterling), inc. service and local taxes. Breakfast is included in European Hotels. Starting from:	
Amsterdam, Netherlands	66.50
Barcelona	41.75
Berlin	38.75
Budapest	29.75
London	37.50
Madrid	31.75
Nice	48.75
Paris	45.50
Prague	17.00
Rome	29.75
Venice, Italy	37.50

Click here for more hot deals

- Click on your destination's link.
- Browse the list, paying special attention to booking restrictions.

- Proceed with booking as per normal.

Pay special attention

If you enter dates outside the posted terms, you may be allowed to continue with your reservation, but at a higher rate rather than the Hot Deals rate. Always check details before booking.

Price bidding

Travellers with flexible dates and a willingness to forgo choosing a specific location, hotel and room category in return for naming their own price, may find the challenges of price bidding are worth the potential savings.

- Type www.priceline.co.uk into the Address bar.
- Click on the **Name Your Own Price** link.

- Review the four steps involved and the tips for bidding, then click **Try it Now**.
- Fill in your travel details and click **Start Saving**.

- Click in the box for the area or areas you are willing to stay in (clicking on the map will enlarge the area for easier viewing), then click **Next**.

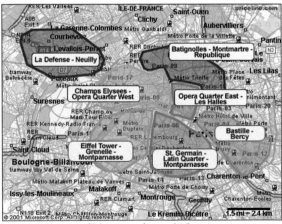

Click on an area for more details.

- Choose the star rating you prefer.

- Enter a bid.

- Type your name in the box and click **Next**.

- Review your details thoroughly.

- Click on the **terms and conditions** link and read carefully before you enter your initials in the box.

- Click **Next**.

| Initial Here: | I have read and agree to abide by the terms and conditions. |

| ‹ PREV | NEXT › |

- Fill in the details form, reading the terms at the bottom of the page carefully.
- Click **Buy My Hotel Room Now.**

● **What Happens Next**

Once you click "Book My Hotel Room", will look for a hotel that is willing to accept your offer price. Your answer will be available at our website in 15 minutes or less.

▢ **If we find a hotel that accepts your price,** we'll immediately purchase your hotel rooms on the credit/debit card you provided to us. Please note, you will not be provided with a list of hotel options. Please remember, once you click "Book My Hotel Room" your request cannot be changed, cancelled, or transferred and refunds are not allowed.

▢ **If your price is not accepted,** we will stop our search and your credit/debit card will not be charged.

[‹ PREV] [**BUY MY HOTEL ROOM NOW ›**]

Remember, this is not a straightforward purchase. Your bid may be declined. If it is accepted you will be notified which location and hotel you have 'won'.

Pay special attention

It is essential you read and fully understand the terms and conditions before you begin, as payment will be taken without further consent once your bid has been accepted. *Be aware that your booking is non-refundable, non-transferable, non-changeable and cannot be cancelled.* See Chapter 5 for more information.

More useful sites:

- **www.biddingfortravel.com** Forum focused on tips for effective price bidding.

- **www.laterooms.com** Last-minute inventory and Big Savers deals.

- **www.travelzoo.co.uk** Directory of Hot Deals and Last Minute Deals. Subscriber only (free).

Your reminder box

• Search for hotels using an online agent, an aggregator or directly through the hotel website.

• Find a holiday villa by searching websites offering inventories in your chosen destination.

• Make a general search for bed and breakfasts, then reserve using the B&B's website.

• Membership in a home exchange website gives you access to homes listed within the group.

• Campsites can be found using a general search in a region or a specific location.

• If you aren't happy with the results list, try using different search terms.

• Check at least four sources (typically, two or more online agents, an aggregator and the accommodation's own website) before booking.

• Hot Deals often yield exceptional savings for travellers whose dates are flexible.

• Price bidding may result in savings, but it is imperative you understand the terms and conditions before submitting your bid.

Chapter 13

Travelling by Road

With so many wonderful destinations within driving distance, enjoyable travel does not have to include a flight or a long rail journey. Travel by road requires a different sort of planning, but the internet is well equipped to help you avoid any pitfalls before you start your engine.

Use it to get driving directions, verify road conditions and check the weather before you go.

Map sites

Whether you need a general location map or driving directions from A to B, Mapquest and Multimap are the websites to get you there. We will use Mapquest to practice.

- Type www.mapquest.co.uk into the Address bar.

- Press **Enter**.

- For a general area map, enter the city name only or the hotel/location address details.

- Click **Get Map**.

- Click the **Directions** tab for driving directions from one place to another.

- For city-to-city directions, type the city names into the boxes provided.

- Click **Get Directions**.

- Driving directions and a map will appear (note time and distance information).

STARTING	London, London, GB	ENDING	Salisbury, Wiltshire, GB		
	Revise | New Directions | Map		Revise | New Directions | Map		

Total Est. Time: 1 Hours, 43 Minutes   **Total Est. Distance:** 88.1 Miles

Manoeuvres	Reverse Route	Distance	Maps
START	1: Start out going NORTH on WHITEHALL/A3212 toward CRAIGS COURT.	<0.1 Miles	Map
←	2: Enter next roundabout and take 2nd exit onto A4.	0.7 Miles	Map
←	3: Turn LEFT onto PICCADILLY/A4. Continue to follow A4. Go through 1 roundabout.	6.4 Miles	Map
↑	4: Stay STRAIGHT to go onto M4.	9.1 Miles	Map
↖	5: Stay LEFT via EXIT 4B toward M3/M23/M40/M1/GATWICK AIRPORT/OXFORD/WATFORD.	0.5 Miles	Map
↖	6: Stay LEFT toward M3/M23/GATWICK AIRPORT.	0.5 Miles	Map
↖	7: Take M25.	6.2 Miles	Map

- Find address-to-address directions by entering full details into the address boxes provided.

- Click **Get Directions**.

- Use the Zoom In/Zoom Out feature when viewing the map.

Don't worry about similar location warnings

If a warning about similar locations appears with no drop-down box for suggested locations, ignore it and click **Get Directions** again. If there is more than one location with your criteria, you will be asked to select the correct one.

More map links:

- **www.mapquest.com** Larger selection of map locations, more features.

- **www.multimap.com** Worldwide maps.

- **www.streetmaps.co.uk** Great Britain road maps. Ability to search by place.

Route planners

Route planners do all the work for you. Enter the required details and they automatically find the best route, tell you how to get there and even point out important features along the way.

Automobile Association route planner

You don't have to be a member to use AA's route planner, an extremely useful tool which gives you the option of listing petrol stations and speed cameras as well as avoiding congestion fee areas, motorways and traffic blackspots.

- Type www.theaa.com into the Address bar.

- Press **Enter**.

- Click on the **Travel** tab at the top of the main page.

- Using the Route Planner box (clicking the Ireland or Europe links if needed) enter your route details.

- Click **Get route**.

- Click on the features you would like added to your search.
- Click **Get route**.

- Driving directions will appear as text.

- Click the **Show on a map** button to generate a route map.
- Click the **Hide map** to return to the text version.

Pay special attention

For more detailed maps throughout your journey, click on the **show map** icon next to each section in the text version.

More route planners:

- **www.rac.co.uk/web/routeplanner** Royal Automobile Club membership not required.

Traffic updates

Checking for live traffic reports prior to departure can save time and stress when travelling by car, even if you are just driving to the airport. If the motorway has become congested or shows unexpected roadworks you can modify your route in advance and avoid a great deal of hassle.

AA offers live traffic updates to help you avoid congestion areas and construction delays while planning your route.

• Type www.theaa.com into the Address bar.

• Press **Enter**.

• Click on the **Travel** tab at the top of the main page.

• Enter your travel details and click **Get route**.

• A links list will appear along the left side of the screen.

• Click on the **AA Roadwatch** link.

• Select a city or region from the drop-down menu.

• Click **Get traffic**.

AA Roadwatch
Last Updated: 17/02/2007 19:16

Road	Incident
M4	Traffic congestion between 4A Heathrow Airport (junction with A4) and J4 Heathrow Spur (junction with A408) in Westbound direction.
A40M	Traffic congestion between North Kensington London (junction with M41) and Marylebone Flyover London (junction with A5) in Northbound direction.
M4	Traffic congestion between J4 Heathrow Spur (junction with A408) and 4A Heathrow Airport (junction with A4) in Eastbound direction.
M1	Traffic congestion between J10A Luton Airport (junction with A1081) and J10 Luton Airport Spur in Southbound direction.
A41	Traffic congestion between Cricklewood London (junction with B510) and Marylebone London (junction with A501) in Southbound direction.
A501	Traffic congestion between Marylebone London (junction with A40M) and Regents Park London (junction with A4201) in Eastbound direction.
A23	Traffic congestion between Kennington London (junction with A202) and Streatham Vale London (junction with A214) in Southbound direction.
M1	Traffic congestion between J10 Luton Airport Spur and J9 Harpenden (junction with A5) in Southbound direction.

- Also try typing "Travel updates" into a Google Search box for more traffic update websites.

More traffic update sites:

- **www.bbc.co.uk/travelnews** BBC traffic updates.

- **www.rac.co.uk/web/trafficnews** Royal Automobile Club.

Weather sites

Your new understanding of searches probably tells you to type "Weather" into a Google Search box. If you added the region you will be travelling in ("weather" Barcelona), well done! Now you will know whether you'll need a jumper, an umbrella or a swimming costume.

Checking the weather

We don't particularly rate one weather site over another, so let's opt for one of the more user-friendly ones as our practice example.

- Type www.bbc.co.uk/weather into the Address bar.

- Press **Enter**.

- Enter a location name or postcode into the UK and World 5 day forecast Search box, then click **Go**.

- You may be taken directly to your destination's forecast, or you may be prompted to select your specific destination from a list of similar locations. If that occurs, you will see a box like this:

- Click on the correct location.

Pay special attention

Forecasts for smaller towns may not be available. Choose a larger city near your destination for the closest results.

More weather links:

- **www.metoffice.gov.uk/weather** Detailed worldwide reports.
- **www.weatherbug.com** US and world locations.

Your reminder box

- Map sites provide general destination maps or allow you to get driving directions from one location to another.

- Try to find out your destination address before you visit a map site.

- Let a route planner do the work for you by suggesting the best way to get from A to B.

- Avoid delays and aggravation by checking live traffic updates before you leave.

- Weather sites are useful not only for knowing what to expect regarding rain or sunshine, but also when it comes to packing appropriate clothing.

Chapter 14

Holiday Health

Travelling abroad presents two distinct challenges when it comes to maintaining your health. First, there may be specific health warnings for the location you will be visiting, requiring vaccinations or medications. Second, there may be regulations or availability issues surrounding medications you are currently taking.

Health advice

Official government offices are an important resource for the most current advice, especially as regards regional health warnings and necessary precautions. They also offer information about travel insurance, medications and more, so be sure to browse through their links.

Foreign and Commonwealth Office

One of the most comprehensive sites for travel health advice is the Foreign & Commonwealth Office website.

- Type www.fco.gov.uk into the Address bar.

- Click on **Travel Advice** under the Services heading in the left-hand column.

- Click on **Travel Health** to generate a drop-down box with several health-related categories and a Travel Health main page.

- Right click on a topic that interests you.

- A pop-up box will appear. Left click on **Open in New Window**.

- Your chosen topic will appear in a new browser window.

Of particular interest are the links to Travel Insurance and Existing Medical Conditions.

UK Department of Health

Advice on health care while travelling, information regarding the EHIC (European Health Insurance Card – for getting medical treatment in the European Economic Area and Switzerland), and more can be found through the UK Department of Health.

• Type www.dh.gov.uk into the Address bar.

• Click on the **Policy and guidance** tab at the top of the screen.

- Click on the **EHIC and Health advice for travellers** link under the Policy and guidance shortcuts heading.

> **Policy and guidance shortcuts**
>
> **Shortcuts to the most frequently visited areas.**
>
> > Health and social care topics
> > Organisation policy
> > Human resources and training
> > Patient choice
> > Patient and public involvement
> > Emergency planning
> > Freedom of Information
> > Performance
> > Medicines, pharmacy and industry
> > International
> > Social services performance assessment
> > Social Services Inspectorate
> > Research and development
> > Information policy
> > Equality and human rights
> > EHIC and Health advice for travellers

- Browse the links to travel-related health topics, clicking on any that interest you.

- Pay particular attention to the EHIC information.

More useful links:

- **www.direct.gov.uk** Includes a section for Over 50s.

- **www.nathnac.org** National Travel Health Network.

- **www.travelhealth.co.uk** General travel health advice.

- **www.who.int/en.** World Health Organization.

Inoculations

If your travel destination requires immunisations beyond standard UK requirements, you may need to begin inoculations and boosters up to six weeks prior to travel. Malaria and other diseases may require preventative medication beginning several weeks in advance.

Fit For Travel

UK-based website including vaccination and medication information for overseas travel.

* Type www.fitfortravel.scot.nhs.uk in the Address bar.

* Click on the appropriate region from the list in the left-hand column.

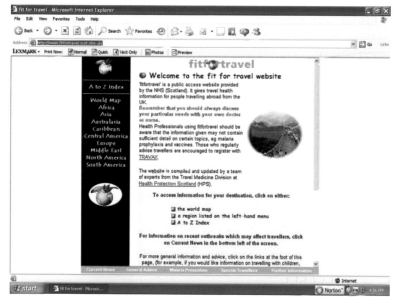

* Click on the destination country.

• Browse the information page for details.

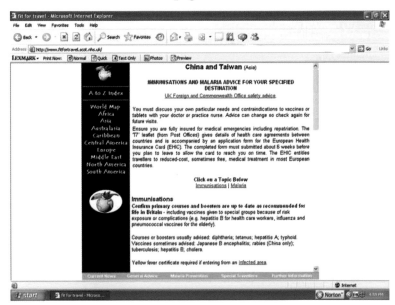

The United States Centers for Disease Control and Prevention also have a user-friendly website with loads of destination-specific vaccination and travel health information. Find them at **www.cdc.gov/travel**.

Pay special attention

Consult your doctor to make sure your medical history does not contraindicate immunisations or preventative medication.

Disabled support

Disability need not restrict your enjoyment of travel and the internet makes it possible to do the careful planning necessary for a comfortable holiday. Knowing in advance what services are available, special facilities your accommodation may include and how to access medical information is the key to a pleasant experience.

Finding disabled traveller health information

General disabled travel information can be found by entering search terms such as "Disabled" Travel or "Accessible Europe" into a Google Search box.

Pay special attention

Make sure your insurance policy or travel insurance covers pre-existing conditions. Be aware that travel insurance often excludes wheelchair coverage.

DirectGov is a good starting point, with an entire section devoted to disabled people, including advice on travel health issues.

- Type www.direct.gov.uk into a Google Search box.

- Click on the **Disabled people** link under People on the main page.

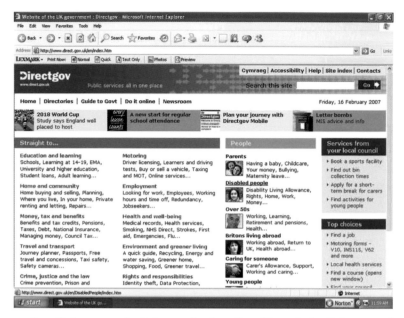

- Scroll down and click on the heading **Travel, holidays and breaks**.

- Click on **Health abroad**.

- Click on the links that interest you within each section.

Spend some time browsing the links on the main Disabled people page for more useful information.

Prescription medications

Whether you take daily prescription medication or the occasional over-the-counter remedy, there are some important considerations to bear in mind when travelling abroad.

In addition to online research, always consult your doctor for advice specific to your medical history and prescription availability overseas.

Travelling with medication

It is always best to travel with enough medication to cover the duration of your stay, plus any travel delays.

Carry an adequate supply of medication in your hand luggage, in the original containers, along with a note from your doctor indicating the nature of your medication and your need for it. This is especially critical if your medication has a narcotic component or if you must transport needles/syringes.

Because security measures fluctuate, it is important to contact your airline regarding current restrictions when carrying medications in hand luggage.

Medication names abroad

Many common over-the-counter and prescription medications are sold under different brand names overseas, and some medications have the same name but are a different product altogether in another country.

If you are concerned about not being able to find familiar medications abroad, it is possible to look up the chemical (generic) name prior to travel. However, it can be a frustrating process and you may want to verify your findings with your doctor, especially if you need comparative prescription names. Your doctor can provide this information if the process described below proves too daunting.

- Type www.pjonline.com into the Address bar.
- Type foreign drug identification into the Search box.

- Click on the **Identification of foreign medicines** link.
- Click on your destination country link.

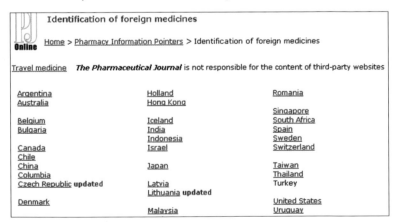

- Your destination country may have more than one link. Click on links which indicate the website is in English.

English	**Philippines** <u>more</u> Department of Health
English	**Philippines** <u>more</u> MIMS
Portuguese	**Portugal** <u>more</u> Prontuário Terapêutico Online
Romanian	**Romania** <u>more</u> National Medicines Agency Product Index
English	**Singapore** <u>more</u> MIMS
English	**South Africa** <u>more</u> South African Electronic Package Inserts
Spanish	**Spain** <u>more</u> Produced by Consejo General De Colegios Oficiales De Farmaceuticos
Swedish	**Sweden** <u>more</u> FASS
Swedish English	**Sweden** <u>more</u> Medical Products Agency

Don't worry **about signing up**

Some websites may require you to become a member. Read the accompanying text, which usually indicates that membership is free.

- Look for a Search box and enter the medication's brand name.

Results vary by website, but if you do get an information page, look for the chemical or generic name of your medication. That is the name you will need when travelling overseas. Brand names differ, but chemical names can help a doctor or pharmacist to find a comparable product if the brand you use is not available.

Don't worry **about poor results**

Even the most common medicines may return a No Results Found page. That does not necessarily mean your medication is not available. Again, consult your doctor for more accurate information.

Travel insurance

If your travels take you overseas, it is important to arrange for travel insurance and again, the internet allows you to comparison shop for the best price, using reputable brokers.

How much insurance do I need?

As a general rule, you will need:

- Medical cover and personal liability of at least £2m for each.

- Cancellation or curtailment cover of at least £3,000.

- Cover on your personal property of around £1,500.

- Additional cover for expensive property.

- Cash and document cover, which will insure your passport and tickets.

- Supplemental Liability Insurance through your car hire firm if you will be driving abroad.

Don't worry about domestic travel

Your regular medical and car insurance cover is usually sufficient for travel in the UK, but double-check with your car insurance company for confirmation.

Finding travel insurance

Simply type *"Travel Insurance"* into a Google Search box and hundreds of companies will offer you their services. Saga are a reputable company that cater to the over 50s, so let's use them as our practice example.

- Type www.saga.co.uk into the Address bar.

- Click on the **Travel Insurance** link on the main page.

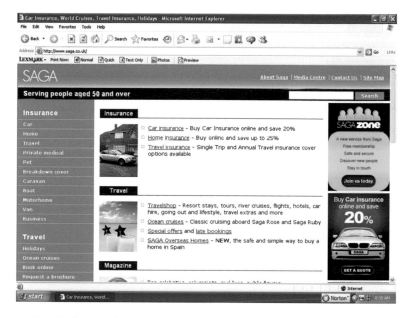

- Scroll down the page to view cover details.
- Click on the **Single Trip** button under Get A Quote.

- Read the important information, then scroll down and answer each question.
- Click **Continue**.
- Fill in your personal details and click **Continue**.
- Fill in your holiday details and click **Get A Quote**.
- Review the policy summary, then click **Buy Now**.

Your Premium £54.00

Buy Now

Please read the policy summary before you buy. We also recommend you read the policy booklet.

- If the cover does not meet your needs, look for the **Start New Quote** link. If it does, proceed with the purchase process.

More travel insurance links:

- www.americanexpress.com/uk
- www.columbusdirect.com
- www.direct-travel.co.uk
- www.norwichunion.com
- www.travelsupermarket.com

Your reminder box

- Check an official health advice site for any warnings about your destination when travelling overseas.
- The European Health Insurance Card has replaced the E111. Applying for an EHIC online is quick and free.
- Immunisations or preventative medications must be started 3-6 weeks prior to travel, if your destination requires them.
- Carry all medications in their original containers, along with a doctor's note indicating what they are and confirming your need for them.
- Medications may have different names or limited availability overseas. Check for comparisons online or with your doctor.
- If you have a pre-existing condition, make sure your insurance or travel insurance policy covers you overseas. Equipment is often excluded.
- You may need Supplemental Liability Insurance if driving in a foreign country.

Chapter 15

Travel Gear and Other Essentials

Whether you need an electrical plug adaptor, a lightweight backpack or a full set of scuba equipment, travel gear websites help you find essential travel accessories as well as quirky little gadgets that just make travel a bit more fun.

Buying travel gear

By now you are familiar with the procedure.

- Type "travel gear" into a Google Search box for general travel-related clothing and accessories.

- If you have specific requirements, use terms such as "ski equipment", luggage or "electric currency converters".

- If you are searching for a specific brand, use terms such as "Scubapro" retail.

Travel clothing and accessories

Use a UK-based website when purchasing travel gear to avoid large shipping fees. If you use a non-UK website, be sure to check shipping terms before ordering.

- Type "travel gear" into a GoogleUK Search box.

- Click on the **pages from the UK** box and press **Enter**.

- For this example, click on the **Travel Gear – Tiso.com** link.

- Browse the links in the left-hand column for any gear or accessories you need.

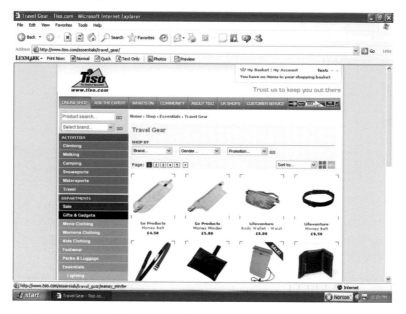

Pay special attention

When purchasing luggage, keep some basic considerations in mind:

- Luggage with wheels is easier to transport than hand-held cases.

- Lightweight luggage allows you to pack more items without going over the airline's weight limit.

- If you are flying within the USA or returning to the UK from America, you need to leave your suitcases *unlocked*. US airport security allows for all luggage to be searched, even after it has been checked in, and locks can be cut off if necessary. If you have a luggage lock, it is best to place it inside your checked luggage until you reach your destination.

Not sure which brand is best? Check out a travel gear forum, such as Travellerspoint (**www.travellerspoint.com/forum.cfm**) for user opinions.

More travel gear sites:

- **www.essentials4travel.com** Includes business-related accessories.

- **www.goplaces.co.uk** Luggage.

- **www.ifsogo.com** Accessories superstore.

- **www.nomadtravel.co.uk** Accessories, traveller's checklist and more.

Electrical plug adaptors

While many travel accessories are unnecessary, you are likely to need an electrical plug adaptor, at the very least. Steve Kropla's Help for World Travellers website has a World Electric Guide listing all plugs you might need when you reach your destination.

- Type www.kropla.com into the Address bar and press **Enter**.

- Click on the **Plug Guide** link under the World Electric Guide heading.

Thanks for visiting this site!		
Please Choose from one of the comprehensive guides below.		
World Wide Phone Guide	**World Electric Guide**	**Internet Roaming Guide**
Use your modem anywhere! Plug Guide	Will it work, and how? Plug Guide	Who are you going to call?
International Dialing Codes	**Telephone/Electrical Accessories**	**World Mobile Phone Guide**
Quick Guide: Calling country to country.	Where to buy the great stuff mentioned here!	Will your mobile work, and how?
Useful Travel Links	**International Cell phones for just $49!**	**World Television Guide**
A list of handy resources.	When you don't make calls you don't pay a cent!	Standards used around the world.
http://kropla.com/index.html Updated 24 December 2006	Fine print and other legal stuff: Privacy Policy Copyright/Usage Policy	Copyright © Steve Kropla 1995-2006 All Rights Reserved

- Scroll down to view the Electric Power Around the World table.

COUNTRY	VOLTAGE	FREQUENCY	PLUG	COMMENTS
Afghanistan	220 V	50 Hz	C & E *	* A UN correspondent reports C and F common in Kabul, but its likely a variety of plugs may be used around the country. Some sources report Type D also in use. Other reports indicate voltage variances from 160V to 280V.
Albania	220 V*	50 Hz	C & F	*Voltage variations common
Algeria	230 V	50 Hz	C* & F	*A variation of Type C with a ground post offset about 1/2-inch from center may also be found.
American Samoa	120 V	60 Hz	A, B, F & I	
Andorra	230 V	50 Hz	C & F	
Angola	220 V	50 Hz	C	
Anguilla	110 V	60 Hz	A (maybe B)	
Antigua	230 V*	60 Hz	A & B	*Airport area is reportedly Antigua power is 110 V.
Argentina	220 V	50 Hz	C & I*	*Neutral and line wires are reversed from that used in Australia and elsewhere. Click here for more.
Armenia	220 V	50 Hz	C & F	
Aruba	127 V*	60 Hz	A, B & F	*Lago Colony 115V
Australia	240 V	50 Hz	I	*Outlets typically controlled by adjacent switch. Click here for more.

Don't worry about plug types

You can purchase kits containing several plug types rather than a single plug adaptor, which is especially useful if you are travelling to more than one country.

Specialist equipment

General travel equipment sites may also offer specialist gear, but certain items are best found through a company that concentrates on a particular type or a specific brand.

Finding speciality items

Your search terms will depend entirely on which speciality items you are looking for.

- Enter the type of equipment ("scuba gear", "cross country skis") or the brand name ("Flexia" dive suits, "Nikon binoculars") into a Google Search box.

- Click in the **pages from the UK** box and press **Enter**.

- Click on the product link or products list that meets your needs.

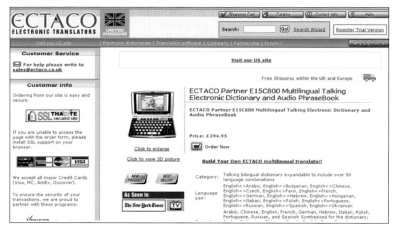

Remember to look for the closed padlock in the bottom right corner of your browser or next to the Address bar to ensure your personal information is secure when ordering.

Don't worry **about what's in stock**

Using brand names in your search terms will result in a list of websites that carry that brand of equipment (though they may also carry several other brands as well) which may save you the time and frustration of searching through numerous sites that don't have what you want.

Phoning from overseas

You're enjoying the holiday of a lifetime and just can't wait to phone the family to tell them about it! Overseas phone calls can be enormously expensive when made from a hotel phone, but, with the help of your internet skills, you can purchase an International calling card, SIM card or pay-as-you-go phone, easing the sting just a bit.

Finding a phone card

International phone cards (pre-paid calling cards) are easy to find online. The tricky part is comparing the dozens of cards on offer. Be sure to read the terms of use carefully as you comparison shop.

* Type "International phone cards" into a Google Search box.

* Click on the **pages from the UK** box and press **Enter**.

For practice, we will use Planet Phone Cards.

* Type www.planetphonecards.com in the Address bar and press **Enter**.

* From the main page, use the **Call Calculator** to view sample rates.

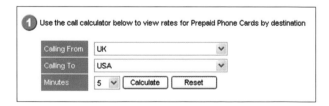

- Or click on the flag of the country you will be calling from to compare cards.

- A list of cards will appear. Click on the **more info** link to view each card's terms of use.

Compare several sites for rates and best terms of use. It can be a frustrating process and you may be tempted to give up and send the grandchildren a postcard instead. But they would rather hear your voice, so stick with it, at least through two or three websites.

Pay special attention

Your mobile phone must be tri-band to make calls from abroad. Check with your service provider to confirm this, or for assistance in setting up an overseas calling option. Bear in mind, even tri-band phones will not work in Japan or South Korea.

Useful links:

• **www.1st4phonecards.com** Phone cards.

• **www.ekall.com/ekit/home** Calling cards.

• **www.reviewcentre.com/products326.html** Phone card reviews.

SIM cards

A SIM card is the small removable device inside your mobile phone that stores your details and allows you to connect to your service provider. Purchasing a Roaming SIM card allows you to make and receive calls abroad for a fraction of the regular calling rate.

• Type "Roaming SIM card" into a GoogleUK Search box.

• Compare rates using three or more websites.

Pay special attention

Your phone must be 'unlocked', meaning your service provider must allow use of a SIM card other than the one that links directly to their service. Your phone may already be unlocked (try using another SIM card in your phone to check. If you can view the menu the phone is unlocked), if not, ask your provider to unlock it. Some providers do not allow unlocking; some just charge for the service.

Useful links:

- **www.gosim.com** International SIM cards.
- **www.mesim.com** SIM cards.
- **www.orate.co.uk/Roaming** Global SIM cards.

Prepaid wireless phone services

Wireless mobile phone service providers purchase network access from established companies, then resell the connection under their own brand name, allowing users to access service internationally on a prepaid or pay-as-you-go basis.

Check details on:

- **www.t-mobile.co.uk**
- **www.tracfone.com/home_page.jsp**
- **www.virginmobile.com/vm/home.do**

Your reminder box

- Consider any special clothing, accessories or equipment you may need during your journey or while on holiday, then search by category or brand name.
- Invest in sturdy, lightweight luggage on wheels, if possible.
- Purchase an electrical power converter for international travel.
- Phone cards, SIM cards or pay-as-you-go phones may save money on overseas calls.
- Confirm that your mobile phone is able to make calls when travelling abroad.

Hopefully, your confidence has soared as you mastered the skills necessary for researching and booking your travel using the internet.

Congratulate yourself – and start packing!

Chapter 16

Reference and Useful Sites

This chapter is organised in alphabetical order so it is easy to find your way around.

Aggregators
http://uk.sidestep.com SideStep
www.kayak.co.uk Kayak
www.kelkoo.co.uk Kelkoo
www.travelsupermarket.com
Travel Supermarket

Air travel
www.airlinequality.com Skytrax
www.cheapflights.co.uk CheapFlights
(aggregator)
www.dialaflight.com Dial-A-Flight
www.flightsdirect.com Flights Direct
www.skyscanner.net Skyscanner

Charter airlines
www.firstchoice.co.uk/flights First
Choice Airways
www.flyastraeus.com Astraeus
www.flythomascook.com Thomas
Cook Airlines
www.monarchcharter.com Monarch
Airlines
www.mytravel.com My Travel
Airways
www.thomsonfly.com Thomsonfly
www.xl.com XL Airways

Low-cost airlines
www.bmibaby.com bmi Baby
www.easyjet.com EasyJet
www.flybe.com flybe
www.flyglobespan.com Globespan
www.flyvlm.com VLM
www.jet2.com Jet2
www.mytravellite.com MyTravel Lite
www.ryanair.com Ryanair
www.virgin-express.com Virgin Express
www.xl.com XL Airways

Scheduled airlines
NB: with some foreign airlines, you may need to look for a link on their home page (usually under Your Region) which re-sets their details relevant to the United Kingdom.
www.aerlingus.com Aer Lingus
www.airfrance.co.uk Air France
www.alitalia.com Alitalia
www.americanairlines.co.uk American
Airlines
www.britishairways.com British
Airways
www.cathaypacific.com Cathay Pacific
Airways
www.continental.com/uk Continental
Airways
www.delta.com Delta Airlines
www.elal.co.il El Al Israel Airlines
www.emirates.com/uk Emirates
www.flybmi.com British Midland (bmi)
www.flysas.com SAS Scandinavian
Airlines
www.gbairways.com GB Airways
www.iberiaairlines.co.uk Iberia
www.klm.co.uk KLM Royal Dutch
Airlines
www.lufthansa.co.uk Lufthansa
www.qantas.com.au Qantas
www.unitedairlines.co.uk United
Airlines
www.usairways.com US Airways
www.virgin-atlantic.com Virgin
Atlantic Airways

Airport parking
www.aph.com Airport Parking and
Hotels
www.holidayextras.co.uk Holiday
Extras

www.parkbcp.co.uk BCP
www.parking4less.co.uk Parking 4 Less
www.purpleparking.com Purple Parking

Bidding sites
www.biddingfortravel.com Bidding
For Travel
www.priceline.co.uk Priceline
www.skyauction.co.uk Skyauction

Car hire
www.alamo.co.uk Alamo
www.avis.co.uk Avis
www.carhire3000.com Carhire 3000
www.carrentals.co.uk Carrentals
www.easycar.com easyCar
www.hertz.co.uk Hertz
www.holidayautos.co.uk Holiday Autos
www.thrifty.co.uk Thrifty Car Rental

Consumer safety
www.consumerdirect.gov.uk
Consumer Direct
www.dti.gov.uk Department of Trade
and Industry
www.getsafeonline.org.uk Get Safe
Online

Cruises
www.cruisedirect.com Cruise Direct
www.cruiseline.co.uk The Cruise Line
agency
www.cunard.com Cunard
www.discover-cruises.co.uk Discover
Cruises
www.easycruise.com easyCruise
www.fredolsencruises.com Fred. Olsen
Cruises
www.islandcruises.com Island Cruises
www.oceanvillageholidays.co.uk
Ocean Village
www.pocruises.com P&O Cruises
www.psa-psara.org Passenger Shipping
Association
www.seaview.co.uk/cruises.asp
Seaview
www.thecruisestore.co.uk The Cruise
Store
www.worldofcruisingmagazine.com/
planner.php *World of Cruising*
magazine

River cruises
www.deilmann.co.uk Peter Deilmann
Cruises
www.gobarging.com European
Waterways
www.majesticamericaline.com Delta
Queen Steamboats
www.orient-express.com Orient
Express
www.vikingcruises.co.uk Viking River
Cruises

Destination information
www.lonelyplanet.com Lonely Planet
www.seniorstravelguide.com Seniors
Travel Guide
www.travel.dk.com Dorling-
Kindersley (DK)
www.travel-advice.net Travel Advice
www.tripadvisor.com Trip Advisor
www.virtualtourist.com Virtual
Tourist

Directories
http://dir.yahoo.com Yahoo directory
www.dmoz.org Open Directory
Project
www.google.com/dirhp Google
directory

Disabled-friendly
www.abletogo.com AbleToGo
www.access-able.com Access Able
Travel Source (American)
www.access-travel.co.uk Access Travel
www.barrheadtravel.co.uk Barrhead
Travel
www.canbedone.co.uk Can Be Done
www.carewellholidays.com Carewell
Holidays
www.chalfont-line.co.uk Chalfont Line
www.direct.gov.uk Directgov
www.disabilitytravel.co.uk Disability
Travel
www.disabledholidayinfo.org.uk
Disabled Holiday Info
www.enableholidays.com Enable
Holidays
www.flying-with-disability.org Flying
with Disability
www.medicaltravel.org Medical Travel
www.radar.co.uk Royal Association for
Disability and Rehabilitation

www.thebigproject.co.uk The Big
Project

Cruise lines
www.accessibletravel.co.uk Accessible
Travel & Leisure
www.cruisecritic.com Cruise Critic
(Discussion forum)
www.cruisingholiday.co.uk Cruising
Holiday
www.hollandamerica.com Holland
America Line
www.princesscruises.co.uk Princess
Cruises
www.royalcaribbean.co.uk Royal
Caribbean International
www.rssc.co.uk Regent Seven Seas
Cruises

Speciality travel
www.bendrigg.org.uk The Bendrigg
Trust
www.brucetrust.org.uk The Bruce
Trust
www.disabilitysnowsport.org.uk
Disability Snowsport UK
www.globetrotterclub.com
GlobeTrotterClub
www.optionsholidays.co.uk Options
Holidays
www.staffordshiremoorlandsfarm
holidays.co.uk Staffordshire
Moorlands Farm Holidays

Discussion forums
www.aardvarktravel.net/chat
Aardvarktravel
www.fodors.com/forums Fodors
www.lonelyplanet.com Thorn Tree
Forums
www.travellerspoint.com/forum.cfm
Travellerspoint
www.tripadvisor.co.uk/ForumHome
Trip Advisor
www.virtualtourist.com Virtual Tourist

Ferries
www.brittany-ferries.com Brittany
Ferries
www.dfds.co.uk DFDS Seaways
www.ferrycrossings-uk.co.uk Ferry
Crossings-UK
www.ferryto.co.uk Cross Channel

Discount Ferry Tickets
www.poferries.com P&O Ferries
www.poirishsea.com P&O Irish Sea
www.seafrance.com Sea France
www.seaview.co.uk/ferries.asp Seaview
www.stenaline.co.uk Stena Line

Guidebooks
www.amazon.co.uk Amazon
www.dorlingkindersley-uk.co.uk
Dorling-Kindersley (DK)
www.fodors.com Fodors
www.foulsham.com Brit's Guide series
www.frommers.com Frommer's
www.lonelyplanet.com Lonely Planet
www.roughguides.com Rough Guides
www.stanfords.co.uk Stanfords

Health advice
www.cdc.gov/travel United States
Centers for Disease Control and
Prevention
www.dh.gov.uk Department of Health
www.direct.gov.uk Directgov
www.fco.gov.uk Foreign &
Commonwealth Office
www.fitfortravel.scot.nhs.uk Fit For
Travel
www.nathnac.org National Travel
Health Network
www.pjonline.com *The Pharmaceutical
Journal* (Great Britain)
www.travelhealth.co.uk Travelhealth
www.who.int/en World Health
Organization

Miscellaneous sites
www.inmyprime.co.uk In My Prime
(for mature people)
www.moneysavingexpert.com Money
Saving Expert (with travel tips)
www.wikipedia.org Wikipedia
(encyclopedia)

Official travel advice
www.direct.gov.uk Directgov
www.fco.gov.uk The Foreign &
Commonwealth Office

Passports/visas
www.thevisacompany.com Visa
Company
www.travcour.com Travcour UK

www.ukpa.gov.uk Home Office
Identity & Passport Service

Rail travel
UK rail travel
www.arrivatrainswales.co.uk Arriva
Trains Wales
www.centraltrains.co.uk Central Trains
www.firstgreatwestern.co.uk First
Great Western
www.firstscotrail.com First Scotrail
www.gner.co.uk GNER
www.nationalrail.co.uk National Rail
www.northernrail.org Northern Rail
www.southeasternrailway.co.uk South
Eastern
www.southwesttrains.co.uk South West
www.thetrainline.com The Trainline
www.virgintrains.co.uk Virgin Trains

Worldwide rail travel
www.eurostar.com Eurostar
www.eurotunnel.com Eurotunnel
www.greatrail.com Great Rail
www.internationaltrainline.com The
Trainline
www.raileurope.co.uk Rail Europe

Road travel
www.googlemaps.co.uk Google Maps
www.mapquest.co.uk Mapquest
www.mapquest.com Mapquest
(American version)
www.multimap.com Multimap
www.rac.co.uk Royal Automobile Club
www.streetmaps.co.uk Streetmaps
(Great Britain)
www.theaa.com Automobile
Association

Search engines
www.uk.ask.com or www.ask.com Ask
www.google.com www.google.co.uk
Google and Google UK
www.holidayhotels.com Holiday
Hotels (hotel specific)
www.ixquick.com Ixquick
www.msn.co.uk Microsoft's UK
default search engine
www.net.gurus.com/search Internet
Gurus
www.search-engines-megalist.com
Search Engine Megalist

www.toorista.com/en Toorista (travel
specific)
www.yahoo.com www.yahoo.co.uk
Yahoo and Yahoo UK

Singles-only holidays
www.adventurecompany.co.uk The
Adventure Company
www.directline-holidays.co.uk
Directline Holidays
www.friendshiptravel.com Friendship
Travel
www.justyou.co.uk Just You
www.kindredspiritstravel.com Kindred
Spirits
www.kuoni.co.uk Kuoni
www.singulartravel.co.uk Singular
Travel
www.solitairhols.co.uk Solitair
www.solosholidays.co.uk Solos
Holidays
www.speedbreaks.co.uk SpeedBreaks
www.travelone.co.uk Travel One
www.travel-quest.co.uk Travel-quest
www.trekamerica.co.uk Trek America
www.turkishcruises.co.uk Day
Dreams Afloat in Turkey

Specialist travel by category
Adventure cruises
www.abercrombiekent.co.uk
Abercrombie & Kent
www.clippercruise.com Clipper Cruise
Line
www.expeditions.com Lindblad
Expeditions
www.noble-caledonia.co.uk Noble
Caledonia

Adventure travel
www.activitiesabroad.com Activities
Abroad
www.adventurecompany.co.uk The
Adventure Company
www.adventuretravel.about.com
About.com
www.canvas.co.uk Canvas Holidays
www.consorttravel.com Consort Travel
www.cruisingholidays.co.uk/river/
steamboat Steamboat River
Adventures
www.crystal-active.co.uk Crystal
Active

www.discover-the-world.co.uk
Discover The World
www.hotels.tv Hotels.tv
www.inntravel.co.uk Inntravel
www.nationalgeographic.com/
adventure National Geographic
www.outdoorfrance.com Outdoor
France
www.sandpiperhols.co.uk Sandpiper
Holidays
www.travel-quest.co.uk Adventure
holiday directory
www.travelsphere.co.uk Travelsphere
www.trekamerica.co.uk Trek America
www.venueholidays.co.uk Venue
Holidays
www.virginholidays.co.uk Virgin
Holidays
www.whydontyou.com Why Don't
You

Arts and crafts
www.allwaysspain.com All Ways
Spain
www.andalucian-adventures.co.uk
Andalucian Adventures
www.craftybreaks.com Waunifor
Crafty Breaks
www.creative-retreat.co.uk The
Creative Retreat
www.farncombeestate.co.uk
Farncombe Estate
www.manorhousehotel.co.uk The
Manor House Hotel

Cycling
www.2wheeltreks.co.uk 2 Wheel
Treks
www.exodus.co.uk Exodus
www.islandcruises.com Island Cruise
Line
www.oceanvillageholidays.com Ocean
Village Cruise Line

Fishing
www.anglers-world.co.uk Anglers
World Holidays
www.go-fishing-worldwide.com Go
Fishing Worldwide
www.uk-fishing-holidays.co.uk UK
Fishing Holidays

Food and drink
www.cookinfrance.com Cook in
France
www.creativitytravel.com Creativity
Travel
www.flavoursholidays.co.uk Flavours
Italian Cookery Holidays
www.gourmet-touring.com Gourmet
Tasting
www.tastingplaces.com Tasting Places

Golden gap year holidays
www.gapyear.com Gapyear.com
www.gapyearsforgrownups.co.uk Real
Gap Years for Grownups
www.goldengapyears.com Golden Gap
Years
www.questoverseas.com/escapes Quest
Escapes
www.singulartravel.co.uk Singular
Travel

Health and well-being
www.banyantree.com Banyantree.com
www.cortijo-romero.co.uk Cortijo
Romero
www.creativeholidays.co.uk Creative
Holidays
www.healthy-option.co.uk Healthy
Options
www.yogatraveller.com Yogatraveller

Hobbies and crafts holidays
www.antiques-safari.co.uk James
Edwards Antiques Safari
www.destinationprovence.co.uk
Destination Provence
www.frenchconnections.co.uk French
Connections
www.ilcollegio.com Il Collegio
www.skyros.com Skyros
www.travel.world.co.uk Travel World
directory

Horse-riding
www.equitour.co.uk Equitour
www.inthesaddle.co.uk In The Saddle
www.ranchamerica.co.uk Ranch
America
www.ranchrider.com Ranch Rider
North American Ranch Holidays

Motor sports
www.1800bepetty.com Richard Petty Driving Experience
www.africasky.co.uk Africa Sky
www.coachtoursinscotland.co.uk CoachToursInScotland
www.forestrally.com Forest Experience Rally School
www.morocco-travel.com The Best of Morocco
www.spaincartours.com Spain Car Tours

Painting
www.bellasardinia.com Bella Sardinia
www.learntopaintinfrance.com Paint in France
www.rileyarts.com Riley Arts

Walking tours
www.aboutargyll.co.uk About Argyll
www.aboveclouds.com Above The Clouds
www.bentstours.com Bents
www.explore.co.uk Explore!
www.pura-aventura.com Pura Adventura

Water sports
www.doggypaddle.com Doggypaddle
www.sunsail.com Sunsail
www.waterbynature.com Water By Nature

Winter sports
www.classicski.co.uk Classic Ski
www.clubmed.co.uk Club Med
www.crystalski.co.uk Crystal
www.neilson.co.uk/ski/index.asp Neilson

Tour operators
www.airtours.co.uk Airtours
www.aito.co.uk Association of Independent Tour Operators
www.aspro.co.uk Aspro Holidays
www.baholidays.com British Airways Holidays
www.cosmos.co.uk Cosmos
www.crestaholidays.co.uk Cresta Holidays
www.directholidays.co.uk Direct Holidays

www.escapades.co.uk Escapades
www.firstchoice.co.uk First Choice
www.funwayholidays.co.uk Funway Holidays
www.inghams.co.uk Inghams
www.kosmar.co.uk Kosmar
www.kuoni.co.uk Kuoni
www.leger.co.uk Leger Holidays
www.panorama.co.uk Panorama
www.saga.co.uk/travel/ Saga Holidays
www.sovereign.com Sovereign Holidays
www.styleholidays.co.uk Style Holidays
www.tcsignature.co.uk Thomas Cook Signature
www.thomascook.co.uk Thomas Cook
www.thomson.co.uk Thomson
www.titantravel.co.uk Titan Travel
www.virginholidays.com Virgin Holidays
www.xl.com XL

Tourist offices
www.europe.org Europe Tourist Office
www.infoplease.com USA State and Territory directory
www.towd.com Tourism Offices Worldwide Directory
www.visitbritain.com Great Britain Official Tourist Office

Travel agents
www.a2btravel.com A2btravel
www.advantage4travel.com Advantage
www.lastminute.com Lastminute
www.airline-network.co.uk Airline Network
www.cheapestflights.co.uk Cheapestflights
www.ebookers.com ebookers
www.expedia.co.uk Expedia
www.firstchoice.co.uk First Choice
www.flightcentre.co.uk Flight Centre
www.hotwire.com Hotwire
www.last-minute-vacation-guide.com Last Minute Vacation Guide
www.mytravel.com My Travel
www.opodo.co.uk Opodo
www.thomascook.com Thomas Cook
www.thomson.co.uk Thomson
www.trailfinders.com Trailfinders
www.travelbag.co.uk Travelbag

www.travelcare.co.uk Travelcare
www.travelocity.co.uk Travelocity
www.worldchoice.co.uk Worldchoice

Travel blogs
www.blogtopsites.com/travel Blog Top
Sites directory
www.IgoUgo.com IgoUgo
www.realtravel.com Real Travel
www.travelblog.org Travelblog
www.travellerspoint.com Travellers
Point

Travel gear
www.travelwithcare.co.uk Travel with
care

Travel insurance
www.americanexpress.com/uk
American Express
www.columbusdirect.com Columbus
Direct
www.comparethemarket.com
CompareTheMarket (aggregator)
www.direct-travel.co.uk Direct Travel
www.moneysupermarket.com
Moneysupermarket
www.norwichunion.com Norwich
Union
www.saga.co.uk Saga

Travel podcasts
www.lonelyplanet.com/podcasts
Lonely Planet
www.podcastdirectory.com/format/
Travel Podcast directory
www.podcasts.net Podcasts.net

Travel reviews
www.britainexpress.com Britain
Express
www.holidaywatchdog.com Holiday
Watchdog

www.iExplore.com iExplore
www.lonelyplanet.com/bluelist Lonely
Planet
www.myholidayreport.com
MyHolidayReport
www.realtravel.com Realtravel
www.tripadvisor.co.uk
www.tripadvisor.com Trip Advisor
www.virtualtourist.com Virtual
Tourist
www.zagat.com Zagat (restaurant
reviews)

Travel webcams
www.bbc.co.uk/webcams BBC
www.camvista.com Camvista
www.googleearth.com Google Earth
www.kroooz-cams.com Kroooz Cams
www.snoweye.com Snoweye (ski
specific)
www.travel-webcams.com Travel-
Webcams
www.webcamgalore.com Webcam
Galore

UK ticket brokers
www.aph.com/information/attraction_
tickets.htm APH
www.attraction-tickets-direct.co.uk
Attraction Tickets Direct
www.attractionworld.com Attraction
World
www.keithprowsetickets.com Keith
Prowse
www.themeparkticketsdirect.com
Theme Park Tickets Direct

Weather
www.bbc.co.uk/weather BBC
www.metoffice.gov.uk/weather Met
Office
www.weatherbug.com WeatherBug

Index